A Guide To Understanding Rad As A Parent

Mia J. Stewart

Introduction

This book serves as a comprehensive resource for parents who are dealing with the challenges of raising a child with Reactive Attachment Disorder (RAD). This guide provides valuable information, insights, and advice to help parents navigate the complexities of RAD and provide the necessary support for their child's well-being.

The guide begins by defining RAD and explaining its characteristics. It addresses the causes and risk factors that contribute to the development of RAD, focusing on the experience of growing up feeling unsafe and how it impacts a child's behavior and emotional development.

Symptoms of RAD are outlined to help parents recognize potential signs and manifestations of the disorder in their child. The process of getting a diagnosis for RAD is discussed, shedding light on how professionals diagnose this condition.

Once a diagnosis is obtained, the guide offers guidance on how to proceed. It introduces the concept of "resetting expectations" and encourages parents to reevaluate their goals and priorities. The trauma-informed approach is explained as a key framework for understanding and addressing the behavior of a child with RAD.

The guide delves into finding appropriate help for children with RAD, including information about psychiatric residential treatment facilities, mental health service providers, medication management, and other treatment options. It provides tips for accessing treatment and dealing with challenges such as false allegations and safety concerns.

The guide also pays attention to the impact of RAD on siblings and offers advice on protecting their well-being. It addresses issues related to adoption dissolution, suicidal ideation, and crisis planning. Self-care for caregivers is emphasized throughout the guide, covering various aspects of a caregiver's life, from relationships and career to everyday challenges.

The guide dispels myths associated with RAD and presents "Ten Ugly Truths You Must Know," providing parents with a candid perspective on the challenges they might face while raising a child with RAD.

Overall, this book offers a wealth of information, practical advice, and emotional support for parents navigating the unique challenges of raising a child with RAD. It serves as a comprehensive resource to help parents understand the disorder, seek appropriate treatment, and provide a nurturing and safe environment for their child's growth and healing.

Contents

WHAT IS RAD?

Reactive Attachment Disorder is a little known, stressor-related mental health disorder caused by early childhood trauma. It's commonly called "RAD" which is pronounced like you'd say, "That's a rad skateboard."

Many traumas can cause RAD, but the most common are abuse, neglect, and abandonment. RAD is extremely rare in the general population but far more common among children who have spent time in foster care or who are adopted.

THE TUG-OF-WAR

If I tell my son to wear blue socks, he'll wear white. If I make his favorite sandwich, he'll toss it in the trash and tell his teacher I sent him to school without any lunch. If I ask him to write his spelling words three times, he won't even pick up his pencil. And there's no negotiation. If I compromise and ask him to write them only once, he'll still refuse.

No matter how inconsequential or mundane the issue is, my son treats everything as if it's life-or-death. He must win at all costs, no matter how long it takes, and despite any consequences he's given or any rewards he's promised.

Kids with RAD have an indefatigable need to control the people and situations around them because they only feel safe when they prove to themselves that they are in control. To understand this, we must go back to the underlying causes of the disorder.

CAUSES AND RISK FACTORS

Let's take a look at what causes RAD and what the risk factors are for developing the disorder.

RAD is caused by adverse childhood experiences (also called ACES) that occur during the early years of a child's life which is when their rapidly developing brain is most vulnerable.

In my son's case, he was neglected before we adopted him out of foster care. ACES also include witnessing domestic violence, having a substance addicted parent, and losing a primary caregiver. You can find a link to more information about ACES in the Additional Resources section of this book.

Adverse experiences can cause "developmental trauma," a term coined by leading trauma expert and researcher Bessel van der Kolk. Depending on the timing, duration, and severity of the adversity, a child can be affected in two key ways.

First, when children experience developmental trauma, they can become "stuck" in chronic survival mode or what's called "fight-flight mode." This happens when the cortisol hormone is automatically triggered and released into the body to prepare an individual to react to danger. That is, danger like having a car speeding towards you as you cross the street or being chased by a dog.

Fight-flight mode is not meant to be a child's "normal." It's not mean to be triggered by your mom asking you to pick up your room or telling you that you can't have a third helping for dinner.

However, for kids with RAD, their fight-flight response is overactive and triggered by minimally threatening situations. For these children, fight-flight becomes a default reaction causing them to be overwrought with anxiety and desperate for control.

For more information on how developmental trauma heightens the fight-flight response, I highly recommend the book, The Body Keeps the Score: Brain, Mind, and Body in the Healing of Trauma, by Kolk.

A second impact of developmental trauma can be interrupted brain development. The human brain develops sequentially beginning with the primitive brain which controls our basic functions including our breathing and heart rate. The limbic brain comes next and regulates behavior, emotions, and attachment. The cortical brain, where we do our critical, abstract, and cause-and-effect thinking, comes online last.

As we discussed, when a child experiences chronic trauma, the stress hormone is released in their brain far more frequently than it should be. This can negatively affect brain development. As a result, these kids can be dysregulated, lack high-level thinking skills, and have other developmental delays and gaps.

For more information on how developmental trauma can impact brain development, I highly recommend the work of leading researcher, Bruce D. Perry including his book, <u>The Boy Who Was Raised as a Dog: from a Child Psychiatrist's Notebook</u>.

GROWING UP FEELING UNSAFE

Developmental trauma can impact a child in many different ways. RAD is a disorder specifically linked to the outcomes when a child's trauma prevents them from attaching to an early caregiver. As a result they grow up feeling unsafe. Let's look at some examples to better understand this.

Imagine sitting down in your favorite chair to read a book. If you're like me you have a coffee in one hand and the book in the other hand. You curl into the chair and begin to read. Do you pause to consider if that chair will hold your weight before you sit down?

I sure don't.

I've sat in chairs tens of thousands of times and in that particular chair hundreds of times. My subconscious mind is well reassured that this specific chair, and most other chairs in general, will hold my weight. As a result, I literally don't give a thought to it.

This is similar to how our children subconsciously internalize feelings of security. When they're well cared for as infants, they develop an innate sense that their caregiver will meet their needs.

When I doted over my babies—making sure they were fed, clean, warm, and cuddled—they couldn't consciously process that experience, but their bodies did. Here's some of what they unconsciously internalized:

- The world is predictable and safe.
- My mother, and therefore other adults. will take care of me.
- I am worthy.
- I am loved.
- I am wanted.

Unfortunately, this is not the experience of all children.

Here are a few traumatic situations. Consider how a baby or young child would process these.

Baby Lilly cries because she's wet and sometimes her mom comes. Other times she leaves Lilly to cry herself to sleep, wet and uncomfortable.

Ben, a toddler, cries because he's hungry. Sometimes his mother is gentle and loving as she feeds him. But other times, her tone of voice is harsh and her fingers press painfully into his skin. Ben never knows which is coming.

Susie's mother suddenly disappears. Forever. This may be due to death, illness, or forcible removal of Susie to foster care. Susie only knows that her mother is inexplicably gone.

Ethan has been physically abused for years. The abuse is confusing, painful, and scary. No one rescues him. No one makes it stop.

In all these examples, these children are helpless, defenseless, powerless, and vulnerable. With their limited cognitive ability, a baby or young child is simply unable to make sense of the trauma as it is happening to them. None-the-less, these experiences become an integral part of who they are.

Here's some of what they might unconsciously internalize:

- No one cares about me.
- I am not loved.
- Adults are unpredictable.
- I am not worthy.
- Adults, even the ones who are sometimes kind, are scary and hurtful.
- I can't trust anyone to take care of me and protect me.
- The world is unpredictable and out of control.

Children who experience early childhood trauma can grow up *without* an inherent sense of being safe and loved. Instead, their psyche internalizes the message that they must take care of themselves because no one else will. The world feels alarmingly unsafe and unpredictable. In some cases, children who experience these types of traumas develop RAD.

Let's look at three common risk factors.

LIVING IN AN ORPHANAGE is extremely detrimental to a child's mental health. Children who are raised from infancy in orphanages —for example, in countries like Ukraine and China—have little to no interaction with adult caregivers. They may have a flat affect with no emotions. After all, they've learned that crying doesn't bring comfort or food. They also do not know how to attach or bond physically or emotionally with others.

LOSING A MOTHER or other primary caregiver at a young age, can result in a child internalizing feelings of abandonment and uncertainty. Many times, this happens when a child is forcibly removed to foster care. This can even be caused by a temporary separation, such as when an infant spends months in NICU or their mother has a serious long-term illness.

ABUSE AND TRAUMA can cause a child's fight-flight mode to become overactive and their brain development to be negatively impacted. These kids are hypervigilant and seem to overreact. This is compounded by their delayed higher level processing brain functions. As a result, they spend the vast majority of their time and energy trying to control the situations and people around them.

Other risk factors for RAD include:

- Frequent changes in caregivers due, for example, to multiple foster care placements

- Separation from a primary caregiver due to a long-term hospitalization of the caregiver or child

- An emotionally unavailable primary caregiver due to the caregiver's alcoholism, postpartum depression, or being the victim of domestic violence

- Spending extended time in institutional care

In summary, kids who experience chronic developmental trauma may not form a healthy attachment to a primary caregiver. When this happens, they grow up without an inherent sense of being safe and loved. Instead, their psyche internalizes the message they must take care of themselves because no one else will. The world feels alarmingly unsafe and unpredictable.

Remember too, these children may be "stuck" in survival mode. They may literally perceive an innocuous situation as threatening and kick into fight-flight mode. Also, their higher-level brain functions like cause-and-effect thinking can be underdeveloped. This is why they cannot be reasoned with or talked down.

While many different types of trauma are risk factors to cause RAD, not all children who experience even extreme trauma develop RAD, although some do.

SYMPTOMS

RAD and its symptoms are directly related to the child not having formed a healthy attachment to an early caregiver. This may manifest in one of two ways—the inhibited or disinhibited types of RAD.

One RAD parent says:

"Why? I just want to understand why my son hates me so much."

Children with the inhibited form of RAD are detached from their caregivers, seemingly indifferent to affection. They are withdrawn and avoid relationships with others. Some are described as having a flat, non-emotional affect.

> Example: A baby who never cries or fusses and does not respond to a caregiver with signs of distress or happiness.

Children with the disinhibited form of RAD are also detached from their caregivers, but they actively thwart affection and bonding (hence the term, "reactive" attachment disorder). They seek attention, do not respect boundaries, and are inappropriately indiscriminate in their interactions with others.

> Example: A school aged child who hugs a stranger they've just met and crawls up onto their lap.

While the "disinhibited" and "inhibited" distinguishers describe the attachment style of the child, there are a number of other symptoms associated with RAD.

RAD is a spectrum disorder. Some children are severely impacted, others less so. Parents anecdotally list food hoarding, violent outbursts, and crazy lying as among the most common symptoms of RAD. However, there is little formal research on just how common each of these symptoms are.

To explore this further, in 2019, I collected data on symptoms exhibited by more than 200 children who have been diagnosed with RAD. Nearly 90% of the children exhibit the symptoms of "crazy lying" and being superficially charming. More than 75% have symptoms of damaging property, poor boundaries, stealing, food issues, and violent outbursts.

While it is disheartening to see how common these symptoms are among our children, it can be reassuring for parents to know that they aren't alone.

Let's dig in a little deeper.

PROLIFIC AND ARBITRARY LYING is one of the most universal RAD symptoms—and one of the most frustrating for caregivers. Many children, with or without RAD, lie to get out of trouble or to get their own way. But kids with RAD seem to lie for no reason at all. That's what makes it particularly frustrating. At 12-years-old, they'll insist they don't know the days of the week. They'll insist they had chicken for dinner when they had pizza. Why?

This "crazy lying" symptomology is likely linked to underdeveloped high-level brain functions and impaired cause-and-effect thinking. The lying can be illogical, nonsensical, about control, or just a fun game.

Unfortunately, it can also be dangerous. In some cases, children make false allegations against their parents which can lead to child protective services investigations, family disruptions, and even criminal charges.

PHYSICAL AGGRESSION in children with RAD is also very

common—and they don't tantrum, they rage. The rage episodes can last up to several hours and include screaming, spitting, and other destructive behaviors.

They've been known to put holes in walls, rip doors off hinges, and climb out of moving vehicles, even at shockingly young ages.

One RAD parent says:

"Has anyone tried putting Plexiglass
between the driver's seat and the back seat
of the car to keep driving safe?"

Children with RAD may hit, kick, and bite siblings, friends, caregivers, and pets. As they get older, this proclivity for violence can become frightening. Some assault family members, peers, pets and others.

These aggressive behaviors are likely underpinned by poor impulse control and dysregulation as well as a heightened fight-flight response.

FOOD HOARDING AND GORGING are also common symptoms exhibited by children with RAD. They are obsessed with food. They may keep a secret hoard under their bed or in another hiding place. They hoard even when given free access to food. Others gorge and then vomit, often in front of their caregivers in order to elicit a response.

One RAD parent says:

"My daughter just stuck her hands down her throat and made herself throw up at the dinner table."

This behavior is often driven by unconscious food insecurity as well as feeling out of control.

PLAYING WITH URINE AND FECES are common among "potty" issues exhibited by some children with RAD. They may urinate and defecate in their bedrooms or as part of a tantrum. Others smear feces on the walls.

These behaviors are often linked to the child's subconscious need to control the situation and people around them, but that's not always the case. Abuse and neglect can cause developmental delays, resulting in late potty training. Or kids may also choose not to use the toilet because of PTSD or other outcomes of the abuse they've suffered.

SUPERFICIALLY CHARMING behavior will convince friends and family that your child with RAD is sweet, charming, and polite. They are adept at triangulating and manipulating the adults around them with amiable and engaging behavior. Because these children have an innate sense of insecurity, they are afraid of authentic relationships and don't know how to attach in a healthy way. They also view relationships as a means to an end because their basic need to survive trumps all. As a result, their relationships are transactional.

MANIPULATIVE BEHAVIORS by children with RAD is some of the most frustrating to caregivers. For example, they may trick their teacher into thinking they haven't been fed breakfast. Most are so uncannily good at this that those adults will believe the child over the parent.

As they get older, they may also use dangerous means and behaviors, such as suicidal actions or self-harming, to manipulate situations.

One RAD parent says:

"My son got upset and wrapped his shirt
around his neck threatening to kill himself.
He [did this because he] didn't want to wash
his hands before dinner."

LACK OF BOUNDARIES by children with RAD is a sign that they do not know how to have a healthy relationship. They view relationships as a means to an end. It may be candy, money, toys, a ride to the mall, or validation that you're the meanest mom in the world. They'll seem to "attach" to teachers, extended family, friends, and even strangers with no regard for social mores. However, these attachments are unlikely to be genuine and are far more likely to be transactional.

A "PISSED OFF" MOM isn't exactly a "symptom" of RAD, but it still belongs on this list. According to one leading clinician who specializes in RAD, a hallmark of the disorder is a "pissed off mom."

Raising a child with extreme behaviors can be infuriating. Day-after-day they clean urine their child has willfully sprayed on the carpet. They endure hours of screaming every single day, for weeks or even months. Especially before their child has been diagnosed, moms are exhausted, desperate, and overwhelmed. They're simply at the end of their ability to cope. To make it worse, they are disbelieved, not supported, judged, and misunderstood. Worse still, they are blamed and shamed when they reach out for help. So, yes, by the time the family is in full blown crisis, mom is "pissed off."

In summary, children who have experienced trauma and develop RAD have an innate sense that the world is unpredictable and unsafe and act out with a subconscious need for control. They struggle with attachment and symptoms including superficially charming, manipulative, controlling and physically aggressive behaviors. RAD is a spectrum disorder and with children on the extreme end of the spectrum, these behaviors can become dangerous to the child and family.

GETTING A DIAGNOSIS

If you suspect your child has RAD, it's time to get a formal evaluation.

It is important to obtain a formal, professional diagnosis because many mental health diagnoses have overlapping symptoms with RAD. Here are just a few of the most common:

Attention-deficit hyperactivity disorder (ADHD)

Oppositional defiant disorder (ODD)

Conduct disorder

Post-traumatic stress disorder (PTSD)

Disinhibited social engagement disorder, and

Mood disorder

It's entirely possible your child has one of these other conditions instead of RAD, and to get the correct treatment you need to know. The symptoms your child is exhibiting could be related to learning disabilities or developmental delays. A proper evaluation will rule out neurological problems, autism, and brain injury. It's also possible that your child has coexisting diagnoses. For example, it's not uncommon for a child to have RAD, ODD, and a learning disability.

As an aside, many children who are ultimately diagnosed with RAD are first diagnosed with ADHD by their pediatrician. Unfortunately, this misdiagnosis will prevent the child from getting appropriate treatment at the earliest age possible. Furthermore, common stimulant medications for ADHD can exacerbate the condition. Of course, if your child does have ADHD, those same medications could be life changing.

All this means, even if the symptoms of RAD fit your child to a "T," getting an accurate diagnosis is critical. Here are a few other important reasons to seek a formal diagnosis.

First, RAD is a very specific disorder and treatments for other conditions are ineffective and counterproductive.

Also, treatments, ranging from outpatient therapy to residential facilities, are expensive. To obtain insurance coverage you'll need a formal diagnosis.

Finally, some children with RAD have benefited from medications. These types of medications will require a diagnosis.

If you suspect that your child may have RAD, be sure to see a psychologist for an official diagnosis.

HOW RAD IS DIAGNOSED

Mental health clinicians make diagnoses based on the Diagnostic and Statistical Manual of Mental Disorders (DSM). This is the handbook containing the descriptions, symptoms, and diagnostic criteria for mental disorders. The latest version is the DSM-V.

Based on the DSM-V, a child must meet the following criteria in order to be diagnosed with RAD:

A. A consistent pattern of inhibited, emotionally withdrawn behavior toward adult caregivers, and

B. A persistent social or emotional disturbance, and

C. The child has experienced a pattern of extremes of insufficient care, and

D. The disturbances in Criterion A began following the lack of adequate care in Criterion C

E. The criteria are not met for autism spectrum disorder,

and

F. The disturbance is evident before age five, and

G. The child has a developmental age of at least nine months

This DSM-V criteria is from The California Evidence-Based Clearinghouse for Child Welfare website. You can find a link to the webpage in the Additional Resources section of this book.

Boiled down, here's the diagnostic criteria that will be used to determine if a RAD diagnosis is appropriate.

> The child has poor attachment to their caregivers and persistent social or emotional disturbances caused by early childhood trauma. These symptoms began before the age of five. The child does not have autism and is at least nine-months-old at the time of diagnosis.

Like other similar disorders, RAD is diagnosed by a mental health clinician based on interviews with the caregiver and child. The caregiver fills out a myriad of forms which are scored to determine if the child meets or does not meet the specific diagnostic criteria. Depending on the child's age they will be taken through various evaluations. In addition, clinicians generally administer an IQ test and other psychological evaluations. Autism screening is standard, as that needs to be ruled out before a RAD diagnosis can be made.

A RAD diagnosis relies heavily on the child's early developmental history. You will be asked about prenatal care, pregnancy complications, labor and delivery, and developmental milestones. This can be tricky if your child is in foster care or has been adopted. Request any available documentation from your agency prior to the evaluation. If you do not have these details documented in writing be sure to verbally recount any information provided to you during the foster/adoption process.

The interviews may take place over one or two appointments, after which the provider will compile the results and create a psychological evaluation. This report will typically include descriptions of each test that was administered and the results, diagnoses, and recommendations.

Remember, this is not merely a "RAD screening." It is a full psychological evaluation. The report will be comprehensive and include any coexisting conditions and diagnoses as well as the potential RAD diagnosis.

A psychologist or psychiatrist is best equipped to make a diagnosis of RAD. Most pediatricians are able to provide a referral to a qualified professional. In addition, the Exceptional Children's departments at local schools frequently refer parents out for evaluations and can recommend clinicians.

It may be difficult to get an appointment with a psychologist or psychiatrist, particularly if you have Medicaid. If your child's behavior warrants it, you can access an immediate evaluation from a psychiatrist by going to your local mental health ER. They typically can provide a referral and help with scheduling a timely follow-up appointment.

In summary, when having your child evaluated for RAD,

- The clinician completing the evaluation will meet with you to gather information about your child's current behaviors.

- You'll be asked about your child's developmental and social history.

- Your child will meet with the clinician alone for his or her testing.

–If your child is in daycare or school, the clinician may ask you to have their teacher fill out forms.

–You'll receive the diagnoses in the form of a report several weeks later.

YOU HAVE A DIAGNOSIS, NOW WHAT?

Ironically, for caregivers, getting a RAD diagnosis is a huge sigh of relief. All the extreme behaviors and incongruous emotional responses begin to make just a little more sense. And, now that you know what's going on, you can do something about it, right?

Unfortunately, no. There are no easy solutions or quick fixes when it comes to RAD.

RAD is a lifelong condition that is challenging to treat. As a parent, however, the RAD diagnosis can be the beginning of a critical paradigm change. Now's the time to take off your "Parenting 101 glasses" and slip on your "RAD glasses." Having a RAD diagnosis and learning as much as you can about the disorder will enable you to begin to see your child's behaviors in a new way. You may be able to better temper your frustration with empathy when you have identified the underlying hurts and issues.

THE CAST OF CHARACTERS
A good starting point is understanding how RAD impacts the family. This disorder is devastating for families. Many marriages do not survive, mothers get PTSD, siblings are abused and traumatized, and the child with RAD loses out on their childhood.

One RAD parent says:

"I just don't know what to do or how to keep my other kids safe. I've lost my family and friends. I've lost my marriage. I feel so alone and defeated."

Sadly, RAD plays out in families in predictable ways with each family member playing a role. Let's take a look at the cast of characters.

THE HURT CHILD has suffered early childhood trauma and, as a result, developed RAD. They are often dysregulated and unable to control their emotions. This spills out into destructive behaviors that can prevent them from developing meaningful relationships with others and too often funnels them into the juvenile justice system.

Unfortunately, the hurt child struggles at school, keeping jobs, and having peer relationships. Because their family does not understand the disorder and cannot manage their behaviors, the child is left feeling unloved and unwelcomed which only compounds the symptoms of the disorder.

THE NURTURING-ENEMY MOM almost always takes the brunt of the behaviors from the hurt child. Kids with RAD target their primary caregiver, normally their mother. Many have been abandoned, neglected, or abused by their biological mother, so they come to see their adoptive or foster mother as the enemy. They actively thwart affection and target the mother with their disruptive behaviors. These moms quickly spiral into depression.

One RAD parent says:

"I'm so tired of being on high alert."

Moms feel isolated and angry. Many report feeling like they've become a different person. Some develop PTSD, anxiety, and depression.

THE DUPED DAD usually has no idea how serious the hurt child's behavior is. Children with RAD are adept at triangulating caregivers to further isolate their target: Mom. In most cases, the dad never witnesses the child's extreme behavior first hand. As a result, he believes the problem lies with the mother. She's overreacting, she's too harsh, she's oversensitive.

One RAD parent says:

"My husband thinks I'm lying. He brings our son candy and treats in the afternoons."

These accusations, and the lack of support, further compound the incredible stress and hurt the mother is feeling. Some marriages are unable to survive.

THE SUFFERING SIBLINGS of a child with RAD are called "glass children" because their parents "look through" them and their needs. They miss soccer practices, birthday parties, and don't get their parent's help with homework. Their needs are routinely overlooked because their parents are overwhelmed trying to deal with the child who has RAD. Like children who are exposed to domestic violence, siblings are traumatized, living in a state of high anxiety, fear, and stress. The child with RAD often bullies or abuses their siblings.

THE CLUELESS FAMILY AND FRIENDS just don't "get it." Unless you've raised a child with RAD, it's impossible to understand the scope and nuances of the disorder. The child with RAD is also superficially charming with outsiders, actively trying to get them to take his or her side. This lack of support from "clueless" family and friends is extremely demoralizing to caregivers.

RESETTING YOUR EXPECTATIONS
Parents of children with RAD feel as though all they're doing is keeping their heads above water—and barely doing that. You need

to know that, if all you do today is survive, you're doing great.

Being reasonable about your expectations on yourself as a parent is key to recognizing your child's successes and keeping your sanity.

As you walk this very challenging journey know that:

RAD is a lifelong condition. Celebrate your child's small successes, realizing they may never fully heal. Like a marathon runner, pace yourself.

A high percentage of children with RAD are ultimately unable to safely live at home. If your child is violent or suicidal, they may need treatment in a residential treatment facility at some point.

This is not a failure on your part. RAD is a preexisting condition caused by early childhood trauma. If there's any blame, it's on the dysfunctional child welfare and mental health systems that aren't providing adequate help and services to vulnerable children and the families who care for them.

There's a serious lack of effective treatment options for RAD. It's very difficult to find therapists and facilities that specialize in RAD and have positive outcomes. Even if you find an amazing, informed therapist, it's going to be a long road.

Most people (friends, family, teachers, and church members) are simply not going to understand. You'll be a pariah and accused of exaggerating the issues you're facing. Carefully choose those who you share with. Gathering a strong support system will be challenging, but is absolutely necessary.

Your child may not achieve the educational and professional dreams you have for them. Each child and family is different, but some reasonable goals may be to graduate from high school with an occupational diploma, get a GED, hold down a job, afford an apartment, master the life skills to live independently, get a driver's license, and avoid criminal behavior and charges.

Here's the truth: You've been tasked with the impossible.

Stop beating yourself up.

You aren't a failure.

RAD is too big of a problem for parents alone to handle. The mental health and child welfare systems fall far short of providing adequate supports and solutions. Now that you know your child has RAD, a very serious condition, it's time to reset your expectations accordingly. This will be key to their success and your mental well-being.

UNDERSTANDING THE BEHAVIOR

The behaviors of children with RAD are appalling, shocking, and deeply disturbing. When we begin to understand the underpinnings of the behaviors, they're equally tragic and heartbreaking.

Children with RAD are often described as defiant, angry, and lacking empathy. While this may be the case, it's important that we look beyond the behaviors to the underlying trauma. This requires a paradigm shift—really getting into their heads to understand their subconscious motivations, fears, and insecurities.

For neglected and abused children, insecurity, fear, and hurt are stamped on the very core of their being—even if they only act this out unconsciously. Their brains are 'stuck' in survival mode and as a result everything is about control because they're afraid, anxious, and uncertain about the world around them and their caregivers.

Kids with RAD often act out because they:

- don't trust adults or authority figures

- have trouble showing empathy or remorse

- are subconsciously afraid to bond with caregivers, and

- have impaired cause-and-effect thinking

The child is usually not aware of why they are acting the way they are and is acting out of subconscious trauma-based feelings. Because of this, therapist say that our kids are not purposely misbehaving. Any parent of a child with RAD knows this is simply not true. The behaviors are both subconsciously motivated and purposeful.

Let's look at an example.

> "My child sneaks into the pantry and stuffs some granola bars down his underwear. He creeps back into his room and hides them under his bed."

This happens to be an example from my own parenting journey. My son's therapist told me what most therapist will say: This was not purposeful behavior and this behavior was not something he could control.

Quite frankly, this is the type of nonsense that makes parents of kids with RAD lose their minds. We all know this isn't true.

Parents, like myself, know children with RAD make a conscious decision when they choose how they will behave. This becomes undeniably obvious as the child gets older and can turn a behavior "on" or "off" in the presence of certain people.

My son *purposely* snuck to the pantry for the granola bars *and* was also *subconsciously* driven by his food insecurity. These two things are not mutually exclusive—children can be both purposeful in their behavior and have subconscious motivations.

Here's where we can get into trouble as parents. The behaviors of our children are so extreme and challenging to deal with that we become overwhelmed and frustrated. We begin to focus exclusively on the "purposeful behavior" side of the equation and forget all about the "subconscious motivation" driving our child. It's that balance we are sometimes missing as parents of kids with RAD.

THE TRAUMA INFORMED APPROACH

Becoming a trauma-informed parent is challenging because effective strategies for children with RAD are counterintuitive. What works with siblings usually won't work with our children who have RAD. For example, kids with RAD don't learn from consequences and rewards. In fact, both backfire spectacularly.

So how can recognizing the root cause of your child's behavior transform how you understand their behaviors?

Let's look at a real-life example from parenting coach Sandi Lerman.

> "My son threw a tantrum and broke his earbuds. Now he's flipped into a full-on rage because his earbuds are broken."

THE GOAL OF TRADITIONAL PARENTING is to help the child understand the consequences of their actions. So, the parent grounds the child or gives them some other consequence for throwing a tantrum. Alternatively, they may simply let the natural consequences apply. In this case, the parent explains that the child can't use their broken earbuds. They might get new ones later, but not today.

When interacting with a child who has RAD, these traditional parenting responses are problematic because they will almost certainly *escalate the situation*. Many children with trauma backgrounds are dysregulated and express intense emotions. To them, not having earbuds can feel like the biggest catastrophe they've ever faced.

This is not logical.

This is not "normal."

This is not reasonable.

But this is the reality.

Our kids' brains, shaped by trauma, don't work the way we expect them to.

Now, let's consider what a trauma-informed response might look like.

THE GOAL OF THERAPEUTIC PARENTING is to help the child regulate, so mom gives the child a spare set of earbuds or sets a time to go buy new ones. The focus is on showing empathy and comforting them. The parent shows the child, through her response that this isn't, in fact, the end of the world. Once the child is calmed down, the parent discusses the triggers for the tantrum and suggests coping skills that the child can use in the future.

A trauma-informed approach takes into account the trauma-related motivations behind the child's behavior. Here are some additional examples of viewing behavior through a trauma-informed lens.

- A child who is throwing a tantrum is emotionally dysregulated

- A child who is manipulating situations is seeking to have their needs met

- A child who is raging is having a fight-flight trauma response

- A child who is willful and defiant is afraid to give up control

- A child who is hoarding food is hypervigilant

Most parents of kids with RAD will argue that the trauma-informed view does not fully account for the motivation behind the behaviors their child exhibits.

For example, they will acknowledge that the motivation behind food hoarding can be an unconscious hypervigilance, but they will rightly say, that's not the full story.

Parents with boots on the ground experience find therapeutic parenting to be frustrating because it seems to take accountability away from their misbehaving child.

These are all totally valid points.

This is where this guide differs from most others out there. I'm not going to pretend therapeutic parenting methods work for all kids with RAD. They certainly can work for kids on the mild end of the RAD spectrum. For kids on the extreme side of the spectrum though, therapeutic parenting methods likely won't work. But they still may be the best strategy and way forward, and here's why.

Therapeutic parenting methods fall short, but traditional parenting methods will have you falling flat on your face.

One RAD parent says:

"Time outs, grounding, spanking... nothing works."

Traditional parenting simply doesn't work. The usefulness of a trauma-informed perspective is more apparent when you consider the ineffectiveness of traditional parenting with kids who have RAD.

One RAD parent says:

"My daughter has been sitting at the table staring at her homework for hours. She refuses to do it."

Strategies that do not work and why

- Behavior modification isn't effective because kids with RAD often lack cause and effect thinking and are not sufficiently motivated by rewards. Furthermore, these tactics convey to the child what is important to the parent. The child can use that information to thwart the parent and gain control of the household.

- Punishments act to reinforce the child's innate sense of worthlessness. The parent and child will find themselves locked in an ineffective cycle of misbehavior and punishment when the parent is punitive.

- Multiple warnings are perceived by the child as weakness and an opportunity to continue misbehavior. These nearly always backfire.

- Reprimanding often provokes an extreme reaction, especially when done publicly because it plays into the child's already low self-esteem and can trigger their internalized self-loathing and anger.

- Zero tolerance policies leave parents with little latitude when the child refuses to comply. Parents may find themselves shocked by the obstinacy of the child who continues to up the ante.

- Focusing on "why" is counterproductive because these children typically lack analytical and abstract thinking skills. Asking why or explaining why is likely to be frustrating for both parent and child.

- Responding emotionally to a child's behavior is unhealthy for the parent and places the child squarely in the driver's seat. When a parent takes a child's behavior personally and becomes provoked to anger, the child is in control.

As you can see, "Parenting 101" simply does not work with kids who have RAD. Those strategies:

- continuously activate your child's fight-flight response system

- create a tug-of-war between you and your child

- give your child opportunities to humiliate you with non-compliance

- give your child the opportunity to exert their (age inappropriate) control time and time again, and

- create frustrating loops with no off ramp for you as a parent

Most importantly, traditional parenting methods and approaches will not result in behavioral changes or compliance, especially as your child gets older. Since this definitely won't work, trauma-informed therapeutic parenting methods can provide a meaningful way forward.

Strategies that do work and why

- Give choices that allow you to maintain control as the parent, while empowering the child. For example, ask if they'd like to do their homework at the kitchen table or on a pillow on the living room floor. By approaching the child this way, you can often distract them from willful disruption and obstinacy.

- Be discrete when discussing matters with the child. Feeling backed into a corner, publicly shamed or teased is likely to trigger a negative, possibly violent reaction.

- Rely upon natural consequences which are best for all children including those with RAD. Always use a neutral or empathetic tone and keep it as simple as possible.

- Side-step power struggles by showing empathy, but not engaging in endless arguments which are usually counterproductive. The child is likely to capitalize on any discussion to thwart the rules. They also may use it as an excuse to escalate the situation.

- Be prepared to remove yourself from the situation if you cannot cope. The extreme behaviors of kids with RAD can be extremely frustrating, overwhelming, and hurtful. It's normal to feel emotional, but when you lose your cool, the child is in control.

None of these strategies are a magic bullet, but especially for kids on the mild end of the spectrum, you may be surprised by how successful they are. And even for kids on the more severe end of the spectrum, they are a way forward.

CHANGING YOUR GOALS AND PRIORITIES
If your child is on the more severe end of the spectrum, and

especially as they move into the teen years, therapeutic parenting will not be enough. You may need to re-evaluate your priorities and goals.

To start with, you don't need to "fix" your child's RAD. You don't need to teach them the consequences of their actions. You don't need to get them into college.

For many RAD parents, getting the child to 18 while keeping everyone safe, is enough. That alone is a monumental success.

This takes a significant mindset shift, but can greatly impact how we address situations with our child.

Let's look at an example.

> "My daughter was vaping in the school bathroom. She got caught but the school isn't suspending her!! She sweet talked the principal and is getting a second chance. I'm going to call the school and demand that she be treated like every other student. She needs consequences to learn."

To start with, in principle, I totally agree with this parent. However, in practice, I do not. And that's where we need to live as RAD parents —what works in practice, not in principle.

Let me ask you this, will this child actually learn from the consequence of being suspended from school? Will they stop vaping?

Very unlikely on both counts.

If anything, they'll use this as a future way to get out of school whenever they like. The child will not care that they have been suspended. They may even be happy about it.

On the other hand, any suspension will have consequences for the rest of the family. Here's the reality of what this suspension may actually look like:

- *You* will have to take time off from work to monitor the child

- *You* will spend all day absolutely miserable, tortured by their behavior

- *Your other children* will be trapped in the resulting toxic home environment

If the suspension isn't going to teach the child and it will only be a punishment for the rest of the family, it's time to reevaluate.

How might our response be different if we have more pragmatic parenting goals? These may be some realistic, pragmatic parenting goals:

✓ Help my child get their high school diploma, fairly earned or not (this will make them more likely to be successful and independent at 18)

✓ Protect my other kids in the home from primary and secondary trauma

✓ Protect my own mental health and stay in a place where I won't do something I regret

With these pragmatic goals, I'd be calling the principal to thank her for not suspending my child. In fact, I'd be using my child's IEP to contest a suspension on the basis that the behavior was related to their disability.

How about chores? If you've been asking your child to take out the trash for months—years—and they still refuse, it's time to rethink that too. First, accept that they're never going to comply. Second, realize that every time you ask, you are picking up that rope in the tug-of-war they want to engage you in. Finally, you're creating an opportunity for them to humiliate you with non-compliance. That doesn't make sense if there's no real hope of the child ever complying anyway.

As a fellow parent of a child with RAD, I know this is a hard pill to swallow. I know this is bad parenting advice—bad advice *if* you had adequate tools and supports for caring for a child with a severe mental health condition. But parents of kids with RAD don't have that.

You don't have the tools to do the job. And, so, you're going to have to hold your nose and make the best of the bad choices you've got available to you. You must be pragmatic about what you *can do* and remember that the physical and mental well-being of the whole family matters, including yours.

FINDING HELP

Unfortunately, navigating the mental health system on behalf of a child with RAD is like traversing hostile territory. There are few treatment centers and therapists that specialize in this area, and even fewer that have positive outcomes. Unfortunately, an unqualified therapist or treatment center can cause more harm than good.

A GLOSSARY TO GET YOU STARTED

One challenge for many parents, is simply knowing where to start. Early on in my journey, I didn't even know what to Google for help. The specifics may be different based on the state or country you live in. Hopefully, though, this will give you a place to start.

BEHAVIORAL HEALTH is what's colloquially called "the psych ward." In your community it could be called the behavioral health hospital or mental health hospital. Your community may have a mental health ER. For inpatient admissions, they may have a mental health ward within a general hospital or utilize mental health hospitals in your area or state. Admission guidelines vary, but at a minimum your child will be seen in the ER if they are a danger to themselves or others. Unfortunately, a mental health ER is often the first stop for help for many of our families.

CRISIS INTERVENTION TEAMS (CITS) are increasingly part of police departments throughout the country. These are teams or officers who are front line responders to people in crisis. This is a collaboration between law enforcement and mental health service providers to employ appropriate response strategies for people in crisis based on signs of mental illness. Typically, you can request a CIT team or officer when you call 911.

DAY TREATMENT is a program available to children who cannot function in a school or daycare setting due to severe mental health needs. These are also called partial hospitalization programs. Services include academics, group and individual therapy and learning coping skills. If your child has Medicaid, it may cover transportation as well. These programs do not offer overnight services. However, your child can be in a residential program and attending day treatment at the same time.

FOSTER CARE is available at different levels based on the needs of the child. Many children with mental health issues end up in a therapeutic level foster home rather than a regular home. It is important to note, if you voluntarily place your child in foster care, you do retain full custody and parental rights. Whether the foster care placement is voluntary or involuntary, you might be required to pay child support.

GROUP HOMES provide round the clock supervision for youth in a home like setting. They have rotating staff and could have anywhere from 4 to 10 children in the home. This is a more structured environment than a foster home, but your child will be exposed to other kids with serious issues.

IN-HOME SERVICES vary but may include having a therapist or a team of workers working directly, one-on-one with your family in your home. The idea is that the team works with the entire family and helps implement the solutions in real-time for better outcomes. For example, instead of an outpatient therapist sending you home with a strategy for dealing with homework time, they will help you implement said strategy in your home.

PSYCHIATRIC RESIDENTIAL TREATMENT FACILITIES (PRTFS) are 24/7 residential placements for a child where they will participate in group, individual therapy, therapeutic activities, academic time, etc. Some PRTF's are locked facilities which is necessary for children who have extremely violent behaviors or may run away.

RESIDENTIAL TREATMENT FACILITIES (RTF) provide residential care for individuals with complex mental health needs. Kids with RAD may receive RTF treatment including partial hospitalization, therapeutic foster care, group home care, psychiatric residential treatment, and long term hospitalization in mental health hospitals.

Mental health services are often bundled under an agency who is considered your child's "clinical home." To find these service providers, Google key words like "mental health outpatient services," "psychiatric residential treatment," and "behavioral health services." You can also get a recommendation from your local mental health hospital.

A commonly asked question about residential treatment is what happens with adoption stipends and disability payments and if the parents will be required to pay child support. Every situation is different based on the agency providing services, where you live, and your health insurance coverage.

In general, per federal policy, adoptive parents do not automatically relinquish adoption stipends if their child is placed in residential care. This is due to the fact that the family continues to provide material support to the child and bring the child home for visits. However, the specific agency you are working with may require turnover of any disability funds and child support payments.

For more information consult an attorney or post adoption services in your county. You can also find a link to an article by the North American Council on Adoptable Children that addresses these specific topics in the Additional Resources section of this book.

MENTAL HEALTH SERVICE PROVIDERS

It is essential to find mental health providers who have experience working with children with RAD or at least attachment issues.

There are a number of ways inexperienced service providers miss the mark with RAD families:

- They offer traditional suggestions and methods that don't work, resulting in frustration and a lack of progress

- They underestimate the child's ability to manipulate and triangulate and waste a whole lot of time in individual therapy

- They discount the extreme nature of the behaviors, placing the child and family in danger

- They believe love is the missing piece and view parents as angry and unreasonable—as the real problem

These types of approaches are, at best, a waste of time. At worst, they exacerbate an already volatile situation.

When looking for a service provider, be sure to ask:

1. What's your experience working with RAD?

2. What positive outcomes have you had with these children and their families?

It's critical to understand that therapists will make assumptions about you and your parenting that will draw their focus away from appropriate interventions for your child.

Here are just a few assumptions they're likely to make about you:

- You need basic parenting instruction and training; you're not managing your child's behavior appropriately

- You're being selfish and need to snap out of it; you're not putting your child's needs first

- You play favorites and treat your birth kids better than your adopted child

- If you don't feel affectionate towards your child, something is wrong with you

- You are mostly, if not entirely, to blame for your child's behavior

Because therapists are making so many assumptions about you from the moment you walk through their door, you need to go in with your guard up.

Be very cautious about sharing sensitive information about yourself with your child's therapist. It's easy to think of them as objective. They're not. If it comes to taking sides, and it will, they're on your child's side. Do not blurt out that you don't feel affectionate towards your child, that you're frustrated, or that you're angry. If you do, that's almost certainly the only thing they'll focus on going forward. They'll conclude that your feelings and actions, not RAD, are the cause of your child's behaviors. If the therapist focuses on "fixing" you, your child will not get the help they desperately need.

Your own feelings of inadequacy and guilt are likely to be your biggest weakness. This will be especially true when your most self-judgmental thoughts are affirmed by the assumptions underlying the advice mental health professionals, inexperienced with RAD, often give.

As parents, we must accept responsibility where appropriate, but it is important to recognize that blaming the parent, especially an adoptive parent, is an easy fallback position for a therapist who is inexperienced with RAD. Lack of progress with your child can be blamed, not on their methods or approach, but on you. It removes any agency and responsibility from your child. It also deflects away from the fact that the mental health community does not have treatments and solutions for RAD and further research is needed in this area.

Parents of kids with RAD, moms in particular, must proactively guard against therapists compounding our own feelings of failure and guilt. For your own mental health, it is important to learn how to reject the blame and shame that will be continuously shot at you. This is going to be a critical skill for you to have because working with therapists and other service providers is extremely demoralizing.

Hypnotherapist, Chel Hamilton, has created a useful visualization technique specifically to help moms of kids with RAD deal with this. You can find it on the raisingdevon.com website under Meditations.

Here are a few insights I've learned from working with my son's many therapists:

1. "Angry" just doesn't work. You must be diplomatic and present in a way the therapist can hear you.

2. You're not going to win. If a therapist doesn't "get it," just move on – unless your goal is to keep your child in

treatment in which case you need to be conciliatory. This is one case where the ends truly do justify the means.

3. They're not going to give you notes or recordings of private sessions with your child. According to the Department of Health and Human Services, your child's right to privacy in this area is protected under the law, yes, even though they are a minor. You can find the HHS website link with this information in the Additional Resources section of this book.

4. Guard against sounding defensive and demanding. This plays into your child's triangulation and makes it too easy for the therapist to write you off as a bad parent.

In the end, listen to the advice you are given and take what's of value, but don't automatically believe everything you are told. Remember that therapists' unmerited assumptions are probably being bolstered by your child's subtle manipulation and triangulation. Not all professionals are knowledgeable enough about RAD to fully understand the situation you are in or to offer a productive way forward.

MEDICATION MANAGEMENT

For some children with RAD, medications are helpful, particularly for coexisting conditions including mood disorders, ADHD, and others.

The best outcomes will be found by working with a licensed psychiatrist. Nurse practitioners and pediatricians may prescribe medications, but usually lack the experience and knowledge needed to address complex mental health needs. Once your child is stabilized on any medications, most pediatricians will continue medication refills, which is more convenient.

Your pediatrician or therapist will be able to refer you to a good psychiatrist. Seeing a psychiatrist for medication management is well worth the wait, money, and inconvenience. If you are unable to get in to see a psychiatrist one way to access this service is through your local mental health ER, both for initial evaluation and a referral.

OTHER TREATMENTS

You may need intensive in-home services or residential care for your child. Most communities have agencies that provide these services: intensive in-home, day treatment, group homes, foster care, PRTF.

To qualify for these levels of care, you typically have to "step up." For example, you must first get outpatient therapy and have your therapist recommend a higher level of care. That will qualify your child for in-home intensive services. If that service is not successful, they will refer you to a higher level of care such as a group home or residential treatment facility.

Learn how the system works in your area and with your insurance. Instead of fighting "the system" use that knowledge to navigate the system more easily.

Also, the key to getting insurance coverage for these treatments is long running documentation.

One RAD parent says:

"Didn't want to get out of the car so she
peed her pants…"

Document all behavioral incidents and symptoms. In particular, document all suicidal and homicidal ideations—most intake evaluations center around if the child is a danger to themself or others. Be meticulous about keeping copies of all evaluations and other documentation you receive from service providers.

Most communities have a hospital with a mental health ward. Larger cities may have a dedicated mental health hospital. Identify services in your area, especially those that treat adolescents. If your child is exhibiting dangerous behavior or is harming himself, immediately take them to the mental health ER or call 911.

TIPS TO ACCESS TREATMENT

It is incredibly challenging to access treatment and most families are in full crisis before they successfully do. Early treatment is imperative for positive outcomes and for the well-being of the entire family. Here are key tips that may help fast track you to getting treatment.

It's all about the money. Finding treatment is exacerbated by health insurance and other payment concerns. If you've adopted a child out of foster care, and were not provided with Medicaid, send your post-adoption worker a copy of your child's psychological report and request that they receive Medicaid. This can be awarded post-adoption, and regardless of the family's income.

Some of the best advice I received was to continue taking my son to the mental health ER even though it was ineffectual. Ultimately, the insurance company determined that putting other services in place would be more cost effective than having us continue to go through the ER.

Acceptance is based on the child being a danger to themselves or others. If there's a bottom line, that's it. Service providers (and insurance companies) don't care about spitting, truancy, screaming fits, or attachment. They definitely do not care how the child's behavior is impacting you mentally or physically. Stay hyper-focused on reporting the danger your child poses to themselves and others, especially siblings in the home.

Another piece of great advice I received in my own journey was to use the word "rage" instead of "tantrum" to describe my son's explosive and violent outbursts. This began to get the attention of admissions evaluators because it flagged for them how serious the situation really was.

Continue to learn all you can about the services in your area. The more you know about how the system works, the better you will be able to navigate it.

OPEN LETTER TO MY CHILD'S THERAPIST

Unfortunately, working with your child's therapists will be one of the most difficult parts of this journey. It certainly was for me. This is an open letter to therapists. You'll find a pdf version available at raisingdevon.com that can be printed or distributed via email.

…

Dear Therapist,

I am desperate for your help. I apologize ahead of time if I seem angry and defensive. I'm just burnt out and afraid you won't understand. My son is completely out of control and nothing works.

I've tried to get help before from therapists and teachers, even police officers, but no one understands. They all think I'm exaggerating, or maybe even lying. My own mother says, "He's just a kid," and can't understand what I'm dealing with is way beyond normal, way beyond safe, and way beyond what I can handle. My son went through trauma at a young age and has been diagnosed with RAD.

I'm not exaggerating when I say my son screams for hours. He's torn his bedroom door off the hinges and put holes in his walls. His siblings are afraid of him. Sometimes I'm afraid he'll burn down the house when I'm asleep.

When you meet my son, he'll look like a very different child than he is with me. You'll think I'm overreacting. I'm not. You see, my son is an expert at triangulating the adults around him. Due to his early trauma, he manages his surroundings and the people in them to feel safe. In doing so, he's good at making everyone think I'm mean and crazy.

Sometimes I start to believe it too.

I have a secret I should probably share with you—it's true that I'm not perfect. I'm very aware of that fact. I've screamed at my son and lately I'm always angry and frustrated. I'm afraid to tell you this because you'll think I'm a bad mom and blame me for everything. Most people blame me for my son's problems. Yet, I'm the one person whose life has been turned inside out and upside down to try to help him.

I've turned into an unhappy, negative, impatient person whom I don't even recognize anymore. Sometimes I wonder if I have post-traumatic stress disorder, but feel stupid suggesting that dealing with a child could cause PTSD. It would be helpful for you to encourage me to get some therapy for myself.

Even though I'm not a perfect mom, I'm still a good mom trying my best. Before we get started, here's what you need to know (because my son will tell you otherwise):

- I feed my son three meals a day, plus snacks.

- I don't hurt my son.

- I'm not the one who rips up his homework and throws it away.

- He locks himself in the closet under the stairs. I don't and wouldn't ever do that to him.

- Our house isn't haunted, he's not best friends with Justin Bieber, and he's not going to live with his birth mom next week.

My son will tell you things in individual therapy that will take up all of our time to untangle. In the meantime, we'll be distracted from working on the really serious problems for which we need your help. This is why I'm going to insist on being present during all therapy sessions. Please understand it's not because I have something to hide. I just want to keep things from getting worse than they already are.

Typical parenting strategies like sticker reward charts don't work for my son. We've already tried all sorts of behavior modification strategies. I can't ignore my son's negative behavior either. I can't just watch him hurt himself, his siblings, or destroy everything we own.

Please understand, our family is in crisis. This is an emergency. We need help and we need it fast. That play therapy you do in the sand…I don't know, maybe it works for some kids–but not for him.

I'm not trying to be unreasonable; I just know what doesn't work. If you don't have experience working with trauma-exposed kids, please refer us to someone who does. I understand this is a very specific and serious issue that not all therapists have expertise in.

I'm willing to do whatever it takes to help my son heal and to fix our family. Please help us.

Sincerely,

A mom of a child with RAD

OPEN LETTER TO FAMILY AND FRIENDS

Unfortunately, most parents of kids with RAD get little support from family and friends. This can make an already challenging situation nearly unbearable.

For a long time, I believed my family and friends were simply choosing to not believe me. It was insulting because I felt they were passing judgement on my character even though they'd known me for years.

Much later, in retrospect, I realized that our daily lives, the challenges we face as parents of kids with RAD, are literally "unbelievable." Our family and friends cannot understand—*cannot* believe— because they have no context for the extreme situation we are in.

To help with this I wrote a reads-like-fiction memoir called, <u>But, He Spit in my Coffee</u>. The book enables our friends and family to "experience for themselves" the nuances of a family in crisis. It's a way for them to "see for themselves" the shocking dysfunctions of the mental health and child welfare systems. You can find it on Amazon and Audible and use it as a tool to educate your family and friends.

Also, here's an open letter to family and friends that you can download from raisingdevon.com. You are welcome to personalize it and use it with your family and friends.

···

Dear Friend,

I've told you before how I'm struggling with my child's behavior but I'm not sure you understand how serious—how desperate—things are.

Here's the unvarnished truth—my child relies on manipulation and melt-downs to control his surroundings. He refuses to follow the simplest of instructions and turns everything into a tug-of-war as if it's a matter of life or death. Every day, all day, I deal with his extreme behavior. He screams, puts holes in walls, urinates on his toys, breaks things, physically assaults me and so much more. I'm doing the best I can but it's frustrating and overwhelming.

Most people, maybe even you, blame me for my child's behavior. This makes me feel even worse. I already blame myself most of the time, especially because I've struggled to bond with him. It's heartbreaking to know he only feigns affection to get something from me. There's not a parenting strategy I haven't tried. Nothing has worked. Often, I feel like a complete failure as a mother and struggle to face each new day.

Fortunately, my child's behavior makes a lot more sense to me now that he's been diagnosed with reactive attachment disorder (RAD). Let me explain. When a child experiences trauma at an early age his brain gets "stuck" in survival mode. He tries to control the surroundings and people around him to feel safe. In his attempt to do so, he is superficially charming, exhibits extreme behaviors, and rejects affection from caregivers. Unfortunately, even with a diagnosis, there are no easy answers or quick treatments.

Even though I work so hard to help my child heal, friends and family often don't believe or support me which is incredibly painful. I understand it's hard for you to imagine the emotional, physical, and mental toll of caring for a child with RAD when you haven't experienced it yourself. And, you can't possibly be expected to know the nuances of the disorder and its impact on families like mine. That's why I'm putting myself out there about the challenges I'm facing.

I wish you could understand how good my child is at manipulating people—how he turns on that sweet, charming side you usually see. In fact, you may never witness a meltdown or even realize he's manipulating you. Yes, he's that good. When you think he's bonding with you, know there's always an end in mind. He may seek candy or toys. The biggest win of all for him, however, is to get you to side with him against me.

Here's how easily it happens—my child is sitting in timeout, looking remorseful as he watches the other kids play. You think I'm too hard on him and say, "He's sorry and promises he'll make better choices next time. How about you give him another chance?" You need to understand there's a lot going on behind the scenes that you simply don't see or know about.

When you undermine me, you inadvertently set back the progress I've made in my already tenuous relationship with my child. The structured consistency—what you feel is too strict—is exactly what my child needs to heal and grow into a healthy, happy and productive adult.

Please know I'm following the advice of therapists and professionals. Strategies for raising a child with RAD are often counterintuitive and, watching from the outside, you may not agree with them. That's okay. But, instead of interfering, would you give me the benefit of the doubt?

Over the years, well-meaning people have said some pretty hurtful things to me, things like:

- All kids have behavioral issues. It's a phase.
  They'll grow out of it.

- He's so sweet. It's hard to believe he does those things.

- Let me tell you what works with my child…

- Have you tried_____?

- I'm sure he didn't do that on purpose.

- A little love and attention is all he needs.

I know these sentiments are meant to be helpful, but here's the thing—my child isn't like yours. He has a very serious disorder. Statements like these minimize our situation as if there are easy solutions that I just haven't tried. Honestly, I'm not looking for advice. What I need most from you is a shoulder to cry on and an ear upon which to vent—without being judged, second-guessed, or not believed.

RAD is a challenging disorder that's difficult to treat so we have a long road ahead of us. Every day is a struggle and I'd love to be able to count on you but not for advice or answers. I just need you to listen and offer encouragement. I know how deeply you care for me and my child and I'm thankful to have you in our lives. I've lost some relationships through this incredibly difficult journey. I don't want to lose you too.

Sincerely,

A parent of a child with RAD

FALSE ALLEGATIONS

Raising a child with RAD can be a dangerous proposition for all those involved and the best approach is a proactive one.

Unfortunately, many children with RAD are capable of making false allegations. A child's allegations, however outrageous or unlikely, will be investigated. This unwarranted disruption and family upheaval is necessary to make sure children who really are abused get the justice and safety they deserve.

However, the consequences of false allegations can be devastating if a child with RAD manages to convince a guidance counselor, therapist, or police officer that they're telling the truth. Parents can unjustly face jail time and even lose custody of all their children.

One RAD parent says:

"CPS just came. I had to put my baby in
their car, kicking and screaming, all because
of lies my adopted daughter told about me."

Here are some steps you can take to protect yourself and your family.

KEEP A DAILY LOG of conversations with social workers and teachers. Write notes after therapy appointments, and document details of any behavioral incidents. Don't only record on the bad days. Log every day, even if it's just what activities you did, what your child ate, and what time he went to bed. The key is to be consistent and document even the mundane. Your log will be much less credible if you only log when an incident occurs.

GATHER DOCUMENTATION to establish a pattern of behavior. Keep school disciplinary records and ask people to follow up on calls with an email. If your child is admitted to a residential treatment program, request the child's records when they are discharged. These documents may have mistakes, or minimize your child's behaviors, so comb through them and request corrections. Discuss any incidents of false allegations with your child during family therapy. Your child may very well admit the truth to their therapist and this can then be documented.

DON'T LOSE YOUR COOL, OR YOUR CREDIBILITY. When a therapist, teacher, or others bring an allegation to your attention, listen. Breathe. Keep the frustrated tone out of your voice, don't jump to defend yourself, and never exaggerate. You will find yourself in many he said/she said situations and your credibility will be everything. A non-defensive response might sound like: "Gosh, I fed Devon eggs and toast this morning, but thanks for letting me know that he told you he hadn't eaten. If he ever does miss breakfast, I'll be sure to email you so we're on the same page. Thanks so much for letting me know."

BE PREPARED FOR CHILD PROTECTIVE SERVICES

Child Protective Services (CPS) plays a vital role in keeping kids safe. For this reason, CPS investigators err on the side of caution to ensure children aren't exposed to harmful situations. Even when allegations are false, caregivers can face lengthy investigations.

Children with RAD may make false allegations in their desperate attempt to control the people and situations around them. Innocent parents and caregivers are often frightened and lack the resources and knowledge to defend themselves and protect the interest of their children.

One RAD parent says:

> "I never imagined my adopted son would lie about me. Now my son has said my husband slammed him against a wall and CPS has opened an investigation. I recorded my son saying he was going to lie about this, but they don't care."

Diane Redleaf is a leading civil rights lawyer for families interacting with the child welfare system. She has extensive experience defending and advocating for parents who face false allegations of child abuse and neglect. Her litigation and legislative advocacy has created due process remedies for wrongly accused family members.

I interviewed Diane and asked how falsely accused parents and caregivers can successfully navigate the child protection system. The information she provided is intended to provide general guidance for wrongly accused parents who are involved in child protective investigations. It does not constitute specific legal advice.

Here's some of what I learned:

- Insist on having a 3rd party present for interviews. If you're home alone, politely suggest an office appointment for the interview.

- Be prepared for commonly asked questions. You can find a list in the Responding to Investigations manual found on the Family Defense Center website. If you have problematic answers (for example, past drug use or mental health treatment), the information may be used against you. Politely decline to answer and seek legal representation.

- There's no clear law on whether or not CPS can speak

to children without parental consent at school. Request that interviews with your child be conducted in a therapeutic setting.

- Video footage is open to interpretation so consider this when deciding if you'll use security cameras in your home.

- Prosecutors can obtain access to social media posts, including those made in private Facebook groups, and use them against you.

- One way to protect your other children is to put into place a short-term guardianship plan.

- If you feel unfairly targeted by CPS and have escalated through the appropriate channels, an option may be to reach out to a legislator or inspector general.

- Finding experienced lawyer to assist in these cases is challenging. One good strategy is to look for those who have experience helping families navigate mental health related situations.

You can find the complete interview "What to do when CPS comes knocking…" with Diane Redleaf at raisingdevon.com. You can find a link to the Responding to Investigations manual referred to by Diane in the Additional Resources section of this book.

KEEPING EVERYONE SAFE

Safety is top of mind for every parent of a child with RAD. Violent outbursts and physical aggression are far too common place in their homes.

One RAD parent says:

"Buying my first door alarm."

Some kids are prone to self-harming behaviors and suicidal ideation. Granted, many times these behaviors are intended to get attention or manipulate a situation, but the danger cannot be ignored. It is critical to have a safety plan in place.

Your therapist or other treatment team members are excellent resources for developing a safety plan.

SAFETY HOLDS

Standard advice is to "ignore" a child's bad behaviors and they'll stop. This simply doesn't work when a child's behavior is dangerous or destructive. Many children up the ante until you are forced to respond.

One RAD parent says:

"I lock up everything (scissors, knives), but
am still terrified. Anything could be a
weapon."

'Holding' or restraining a child is sometimes necessary. You must be very cautious as this can be both dangerous and abusive if done incorrectly. For example, never wrap your child in a blanket, as there is a suffocation risk. Never lock your child in a bedroom, as this is a fire hazard.

The only restraint option I've used is one I was trained to do by a licensed social worker. I call it a "bear hug."

In a sitting position, with my son in front of me, I hugged him from behind, holding his wrists, and crossing his arms over his chest. I would wrap my legs around his waist to control his legs. I always had to watch out for head butting! I only did this as a last resort and when my child was completely out-of-control—when his behavior was dangerous.

Before you try this, or any other physical restraint with your child, seek advice and training from a licensed professional. And most importantly, if your child doesn't calm down after a couple of minutes, know that you are in over your head. You cannot keep them safe and you need to seek professional help.

KNOW YOUR LOCAL RESOURCES

If your child is a serious threat to others or is threatening to harm themselves, it is best to always act with caution. You may need to call in assistance or take your child to the ER, ideally a mental health ER.

Be prepared:

- Find out if your community has a mobile crisis line and program the number into your phone.

- Know how to contact the police and if they have a CIT. While the police are unlikely to act, their arrival alone can sometimes quickly deescalate a child in crisis.

- Know where your local mental health hospital is and how to do an emergency intake.

- Keep a folder or manila envelope with photocopies of important documentation ready: birth certificate, health insurance card, list of current medications and dosages, name and contact information for pediatricians, therapists, and others involved in your child's treatment.

PROTECT SIBLINGS

Siblings are often direct targets of their sibling who has RAD. If not, they are almost certainly affected by the unhealthy situation they are living in. The dysregulation and other challenges of RAD restrict family activities, cause stress and chaos, and require a disproportionate amount of parental attention and energy.

Siblings are too often collateral damage and the overlooked victims of the disorder.

SIBLINGS OF KIDS WITH RAD ARE LIVING IN FEAR. Many siblings are trapped in a perpetual state of anxiety and vigilance, fearful for their own safety and the safety of their parents.

One RAD parent says:

"My two other kids sleep in my bed with me because they're so terrified of their brother."

Siblings are targeted with physical aggression and witness terrifying situations.

What you can do:

- It's not luxury for the sibling of a child with RAD to have his or her own bedroom: it's an absolute must.

- Put keyed locks on siblings' bedroom doors to help them feel safe.

- Give siblings the option of sleeping on a daybed in your bedroom.

- Make a concerted effort to minimize siblings' exposure to violence and danger by instituting an escape plan for use during escalating situations. Use options like going outside to play, locking themselves in a bedroom (preferably one with access to a bathroom), or calling Grandma to be picked up.

SIBLINGS OF KIDS WITH RAD ARE INTERNALIZING DYSFUNCTION. For many siblings, family life is highly dysfunctional and confusing. This can lead to a warped view of normal family relationships with devastating, lifelong impact. Siblings also struggle to differentiate the person from the disorder and come to hate their brother or sister who has RAD.

What you can do:

- Let siblings be honest about their feelings and don't minimize their emotions or experiences.

- Find a good therapist who can help siblings process and gain some perspective on what they are witnessing and experiencing.

- Rely on an outside person, like a therapist, to help

siblings develop empathy and compassion while also maintaining healthy boundaries.

SIBLINGS OF KIDS WITH RAD ARE LOSING OUT ON THEIR CHILDHOOD. Siblings of children with RAD don't live carefree lives. They miss basketball practice and piano lessons when their sibling flips into a RAD-triggered rage. They aren't able to go on family vacations and outings are cut short. Their treasures and toys are broken. Their allowance is stolen. For them, growing up is full of heartache and challenges.

Living in a home with a child who has RAD, especially on the more severe end of the spectrum, can cause anxiety, PTSD, and other mental health issues. Siblings may develop low self-esteem, sleep disturbances, and perform poorly in school. In additional they may normalize unhealthy ways of coping and relating and carry that into their own future relationships.

This is why it is critical that we do not lose sight of siblings and that their well-being remains as important as the well-being of the child with RAD.

You can find more information on this from RAD Advocates and LifeSpan Trauma Consulting in "The Spread of Trauma: When RAD Siblings Develop PSTD," in the Additional Resources section of this book.

What you can do:

- Enlist family and friends to help with rides to practice, science fair projects, and other important activities.

- When accommodations cannot be made, acknowledge and validate siblings' feelings.

- Enroll siblings in camps; let them stay with Grandma or Auntie for long vacations to get a break and enjoy childhood.

- When assessing residential treatment options for your child with RAD, always be mindful of the needs of siblings.

Many parents are so consumed with the minute-by-minute challenges of raising a child with RAD that they underestimate the impact on siblings. Don't make the mistake of imagining siblings are coping and doing okay.

There are no perfect answers but understanding the impact on siblings is a good starting place.

WHEN RESIDENTIAL IS THE BEST OPTION

While RTFs are rarely helpful for kids with RAD, they can be the best option.

My son Devon was 10-years-old when I dropped him off at an RTF for the first time. I knew almost instantly it wasn't going to work. They didn't believe in consequences. School work was optional. With unlimited dessert and no rules, it was more like a summer camp than a program for kids with severe behavioral problems.

I called my sister for advice and my words came out around a sob, "He's going to get worse here."

"Without hesitation, my sister said, "You have to get him out of your house. Nothing else matters right now."

"But he'll see this as a reward," I'd said.

"I don't care if it's Disney World. We'll deal with that later. Leave him," my sister said.

And I did.

My sister was right. I could no longer keep Devon and his siblings safe and I'd long passed my ability to cope. Devon's behavior had been growing increasingly unmanageable and dangerous. He was having violent outburst every day and the stress level in our house was toxic for everyone. My youngest son, who was four-years-old, was especially frightened and would tremble with fear when he sensed Devon's anger mounting. I was suffering from PTSD, though I didn't realize it at the time.

As I'd predicted, Devon's behaviors did become dramatically worse at the RTF. However, in retrospect, it was still the best option available to us.

Unfortunately, if you've exhausted outpatient options and your child is unsafe, an RTF may be your best option too.

RTF'S DON'T WORK for kids with RAD and it's important to know this and have realistic expectations going in. These facilities are rarely effective for kids with RAD. In fact, they can exacerbate the symptoms, and here's why.

The treatment is not specialized for RAD. Your child will be placed with kids who have a variety of issues including anxiety disorders, eating disorders and PTSD. The coping skills they will learn—like taking deep breaths, playing with a stress ball and counting to ten—are not enough to heal the brain injury caused by developmental trauma.

The workers are undertrained, overworked, and underpaid. Your child will work with a licensed clinician for therapy. Yet, the general supervision is typically provided by workers who only have a high school diploma and on-the-job training. Our kids are very challenging to deal with and the chronic understaffing and inadequate training results in inconsistent quality of care.

The staffing structure lends itself to triangulation. Because workers are rotated (and have high turnover) they are easily triangulated, especially against the parents. Unfortunately, your child will gain a sense of control by behaving this way—a feeling they unconsciously crave—and will continue even when it sabotages their treatment.

The kids become institutionalized. In these facilities, your child will be exposed to and influenced by kids who have sexualized behaviors, use horrific language, and are physically violent. They'll quickly learn the ropes and how to work the system to their advantage, for example, by making false allegations to retaliate against staff or peers. This is knowledge they'll ultimately use to manipulate the staff, and you as well.

RTFs are intended to teach your child how to cope and let them "practice" good behavior for when they return home. Yet, the artificial environment and behavior-based modification techniques do not help them to truly heal.

"Kids with RAD learn to work within the external structure of residential treatment facilities. It doesn't get internalized for them though," says Forrest Lien, LCSW, of Lifespan Trauma Consulting. "Ultimately, most kids go back into their families and fall apart. Sadly, [RTF is] oftentimes the only option for parents."

It's important to have realistic expectations when making this decision. Know that, unless you are able to send your child to a program that is highly specialized for developmental trauma, your child is unlikely to get better. Also know that RTF still may be the right decision for your family.

RTF MAY BE YOUR BEST OPTION even though they don't work. Whether or not to send a child to an RTF is a very personal decision and every child and family is different.

Here are reasons to consider an RTF.

Consider an RTF if your child is unsafe to himself or others.
Remember to consider not only the physical, but also psychological
well-being, of other children in the home.

Consider an RTF if you are at your breaking point. You cannot
help your child when you are unstable yourself. An RTF may be the
breather you need to regain perspective.

Consider an RTF if your child engages in unlawful behavior. An
RTF is a better option than juvenile detention where your child will
get a criminal record and receive little treatment.

The decision to send your child to an RTF should be a last resort,
but you alone are not able to heal developmental trauma any more
than you can set your child's arm or cure his leukemia. All you can
do is access the best possible treatments available and support and
love your child through the process. Do yourself a favor and grapple
with this before you are faced with the decision.

ADOPTION DISSOLUTION

Unfortunately, adoption dissolutions are far more common than most
people realize. This is not widely discussed because adoptive
parents are blamed for dissolutions and feel overwhelming guilt and
shame for even considering dissolution, much less going through
with it.

Adoption dissolution is considered by parents of kids with RAD for
reasons including:

- The family cannot afford the expensive,
  necessary residential treatment that the child
  needs.

- The child is dangerous to themselves or others in
  the family, and the caregivers cannot keep
  everyone safe.

- The caregivers have reached the limit of their abilities after years of suffering and sacrifice and do not have the mental and/or physical capacity to continue.

- The child with RAD has sexually abused, or otherwise abused, other children in the home and the caregivers are unable to provide the necessary 24/7 supervision.

- The caregivers are no longer able to provide a healthy, nurturing environment for the child with RAD.

In all these cases it's critical to notice who is NOT at fault:

- The child with RAD is NOT at fault. The child is a victim of early childhood trauma who has not been able to access appropriate treatments.

- The caregivers are NOT at fault. They jumped into caring for this child heart first without being given adequate preparation. Now, they're not able to access support and treatments.

Mom and Dad, you are not at fault if the adoption fails. The fault for these types of dissolutions lies squarely on the mental health and child welfare systems that do not have effective treatments for RAD and are not providing adequate supports to families.

Do not allow anyone to shame you for considering dissolution. If it is best for you, it is almost certainly best for your child as well. A family in crisis is as damaging and harmful to the child as it is to the caregivers. As a society we used to advocate that couples "stay together for the kids." We now know that can be far more harmful for children than to go through their parent's divorce. The same is true here. If the home environment has become unhealthy and toxic, it may be better for the child to go through adoption dissolution than continue to live in the family.

That said, adoption dissolution is yet another rejection for an already hurting child. Families should always consider all options to avoid dissolution such as accessing residential treatment whenever possible.

If you are in the position of considering a dissolution, consult with a qualified adoption attorney and do not attempt to rehome the child yourself. There are serious legal consequences to relinquishment for you and for your child. It is imperative to go through the processes legally and respectfully.

SUICIDAL IDEATION

It's a complicated scenario faced by many parents—kids with RAD are willing to up the ante sky-high, even threatening self-harm and suicide.

While there are certainly some who are actually suicidal, it's not uncommon for kids with RAD to use these behaviors like a coping mechanism, with no genuine intention of harming themselves. And, the payoff is huge. They avoid consequences, side-step difficult conversations, garner sympathy and attention, and gain control of virtually any situation.

Some kids routinely threaten to kill themselves over the smallest of triggers: breakfast cereal they don't like, being told no, or having to wait their turn.

The attempts may seem melodramatic like trying to slit their wrists with paper cuts. Or they may try to hang themselves with belts, strangle themselves with shirts, or overdose on pills.

During the subsequent suicide assessments (by school counselors or mental health clinicians) it's not uncommon for kids with RAD to admit that they were bored, mad, or frustrated and not actually wanting to kill or hurt themselves. However, the attempts are inherently dangerous, regardless of the child's motivation or intentions.

As an aside, parents sometimes get tangled up in the terminology and insist to service providers that our children are not "suicidal." This is often true, but they are having "suicidal ideations" which are suicidal thoughts and preoccupations.

Not everyone with suicidal ideations has a plan or actually tries to kill themselves. Communication here is critical, so understand that mental health clinicians and other professionals are usually referring to suicidal ideations. Whether your child is truly intending to follow through on their suicidal threats or not, they are in fact having suicidal ideations.

BUT WHY DO THEY DO THIS? In some cases, the behavior is deliberate and calculated. Remember, kids who have RAD are desperate to control the people and situations around them. Other times, it's caused by dysregulation, lack of cause-and-effect thinking, and poor impulse control. More often than not, many of these factors are at play.

In these situations, it's helpful to remember that our child's innate need to control situations and people is borne of childhood trauma. We are better positioned to react from a place of empathy when we keep in mind the neglect or abuse that has caused our child to go to such desperate lengths.

Though the initial incidents of suicidal ideation are alarming, parents of kids with RAD can become weary and calloused over time. It is, after all, counterintuitive to give credence to threats that seem designed to manipulate or control, but these behaviors are simply too serious to ever be minimized or ignored.

Even if you're 100% certain that your child has no intention to kill himself, you must take suicidal ideations seriously every time. Here's why.

1. You may be misinterpreting the situation and they may truly desire to harm themselves.

2. They can accidentally hurt themselves, even if that's not their intention.

3. These behaviors are clearly indicative of an underlying problem that needs to be addressed.

If your child is having suicidal ideations here are some steps you can take to keep them safe and find a way forward.

PLAN AHEAD

- Create a detailed safety plan.

- Know what mental health resources are available in your area including contact information, hours, and crisis services offered.

- Be vigilant. What this looks like in your home will be unique to your situation, but it may include locking away knives, removing belts, or installing collapsing closet rods.

IN THE MOMENT

- Deescalate the situation at all costs in order to stop your child from endangering themselves.

- Lower your expectations. Now's not the time to quibble about tone of voice, cursing, and other unacceptable behaviors. Your only goal is to keep your child safe.

- Seek emergency help by calling a crisis team or taking your child to the mental health ER. In some cases, you can schedule an emergency session with an outpatient therapist.

AFTER THE FACT

- Follow-through with recommendations for therapy, medication management, and other services.

- Identify and address underlying triggers.

- Update your safety plan based on the episode.

When our children use suicidal ideations to manipulate and control situations it can become tiresome and frustrating. That's the reality of parenting a child with RAD. It's easy to begin reacting to these behaviors like we do any other attention-seeking behavior. But, with suicidal ideation the risks are simply too high. Always take suicidal ideations seriously and make safety your priority.

TAKE CARE OF YOURSELF

Navigating the challenges and stress of caring for a child with RAD can make feelings of depression, anxiety, agitation, and frustration start to feel normal. Parents of kids with RAD put self-care on the back burner or neglect it altogether while in perpetual crisis mode.

To be effective, parents need to take care of themselves. The child can't begin to heal while their family is falling apart. That's a lose-lose for everyone.

RAISING YOUR RESILIENCE

As parents of children with RAD, life can be so stressful it feels impossible to face another day. Our instinct is to imagine that finding a way to "fix" our child will immediately relieve the stress we are experiencing. In reality, as necessary as it is, getting help for our child adds more stress to our lives because it comes with therapy appointments, challenging therapeutic parenting approaches, and disputes with insurance companies.

Raising, finding help for, and advocating for a child with RAD is difficult. It's stressful. Parents get PTSD, become depressed, and struggle with other mental health issues. They lose friends and family, and turn into someone they feel they don't even know. This is why we need to find ways to increase our resilience.

One RAD parent says:

"I used to be fun, happy, and a good mom.
Now I feel like a complete failure. I'm a
mess."

Adoptive parent and co-host of *The Adoption & Fostering Podcast*,

Al Coates, is flipping the paradigm by focusing on practical ways we as parents can increase our resilience—our ability to take whatever's thrown our way, figuratively and literally. With his background in social work, Al has taken the *Stress-Vulnerability Model* developed in 2002 by Professor Alison Brabban and Dr. Douglas Tukington and tweaked it specifically for parents who are raising kids with challenging behaviors and complex mental health needs.

To understand the *Stress-Vulnerability Model* let's start by imagining a bucket. Inside the bucket are your stressors. Each stressor is like a cupful of water that's filling your bucket up. For now, we'll set aside the stress specifically related to parenting a child of RAD. Instead, let's focus on the stressors that are with you before you even start your day.

MONEY
Are you scraping by and just making ends meet, worried about retirement, or struggling to pay the mortgage?

CAREER
Are you in a job that's unfulfilling, or perhaps you are under a great deal of stress with deadlines and frustrated customers?

RELATIONSHIPS
Is your relationship with your spouse strained or do you have a toxic friend or family member in your life?

OTHER CHILDREN
Do you have a special needs child who requires extra help, or a high school football player that needs to get to practice on time five days a week?

EVERYDAY NUISANCES

How about that neighbor's dog that barks like crazy, or an air-conditioner that's on the fritz, leaving you hot and sweaty?

SOCIAL HISTORY
Do you have a personal history of neglect or abuse, something that is easily triggered?

MEDICAL
Are you the kind of person who needs eight hours sleep or someone who has debilitating migraines?

Think of each of these stressors as a cup of water in your bucket. It's easy to see how we wake up with our bucket already almost full. And if your bucket is already nearly full, you simply don't have room for a temper tantrum, a broken window, or a screaming child.

That's how we reach our tipping point. Our stress-level is already so high that we can't handle even one more thing. And what sloshes out, over the side of our bucket, is anger, frustration, tears, and more.

Now imagine how much better you could cope if you started your day with your bucket only half full. You'd have a whole lot more to give your kids in terms of time, energy, and patience. You'd be a more resilient parent, better able to weather the storms that come your way.

So how can we begin to reduce our normal stress to increase our resilience?

Create a personal list of stressors and solutions. Using the list above as a starting point, write down the stressors in your life and possible solutions. For example, one of my stressors is a propensity for migraines. One solution would be to set a cell phone alarm so I remember to take my preventative medications. Another would be to set autofill with my pharmacy on my rescue medication so I'm never out.

Go for the low hanging fruit first. Start by picking off the stressors that are easy to address. For me, that might mean asking a teammate to give my son a ride home from football practice. Look for quick and easy ways, like this, to take a scoop of stress out of your bucket.

Set some longer-term goals. Other changes are more difficult to make such as changing jobs or affording a new air conditioner (although a rotating fan or two might be a short-term solution). Don't stress yourself out trying to de-stress by taking on too much at one time. Pick one goal at a time to focus on.

Remember change takes time. But, every cupful of stress relief is one less cup in your bucket. It gives you the space in your bucket to handle stressors that might come your way which makes you more resilient. Even small changes will make a difference.

Another way to build your resilience is to increase your stress tolerance. Not all our buckets are the same size. Some of us have short buckets—stress is very difficult for us to handle. Some of us have tall buckets—we can tolerate higher levels of stress. This is your stress tolerance.

Here are just a few strategies to get you started increasing your stress tolerance.

- Get your endorphins pumping even if the only exercise you can fit in is walking the track while you're parked in carpool line waiting for the afternoon bell.

- Eat well and stay hydrated to significantly boost your mood and energy.

- Practice relaxation techniques like breathing exercises, meditation, and aromatherapy.

- Take care of yourself. It's not as impossible as you might think. Up next, we'll go through a self-care list that's realistic for parents in our challenging situations.

SELF-CARE LIST

Typical parenting self-care lists include weekend getaways, yoga classes, 5K training, nine hours of sleep a night, healthy eating, and meditation. What!? For a parent of a child with RAD, these ideas are woefully out of touch with our day-to-day reality.

Parents of children with RAD need simple, realistic ways to begin to care for themselves. So, here's a self-care list curated specifically for exhausted, frazzled, frustrated parents.

Buy little indulgences to calm you.

Nestle scented candles strategically throughout your home to provide scents for instant relaxation and calm. Pamper yourself with essential oils to make the most of your shower (perhaps one of the few moments of privacy you get).

Use simple tricks to feel better physically.

Splurge on a really great refillable water bottle and stay hydrated to improve your overall energy and health. Stock up on grab-and-go healthy snacks (but don't beat yourself up when you grab for a high-carb, high-satisfaction treat during a rough patch).

Look for support in the nooks and crannies of life.

Fill up your social media feeds with encouragement at your fingertips by following pages, people, and accounts that post motivational quotes and memes. My Facebook page @RaisingDevon is just one.

make up for activities you don't have time for anymore.
Don't miss out on your favorite shows. Use DVR to enjoy them when you can sneak a few moments to yourself.

Listen to short meditations.
Check out the free Meditation Minis podcast by Chel Hamilton to relax, de-stress, and fall asleep faster. They're about 10 minutes long—a perfect length for busy parents of kids with RAD.

Seek the small feel-good moments.
Open your curtains and let natural light nurture your mood and improve your concentration. Get your endorphins pumping by walking laps while your child is occupied in baseball, soccer, or football practice.

Make those few hours of sleep you get as rejuvenating as possible.
Purchase a pillow that provides good support. Check out a weighted stress blanket . Find recommendations for my favorite in the Additional Resources section of this book.

Don't sacrifice your daily coffee even on the most chaotic of mornings.
This one is an absolute must for me! Use the app for your local coffee shop to order ahead and skip the line. (I use online apps to order ahead and earn rewards too.)

Pamper yourself.
Get a pedicure or manicure. Just a glimpse of my strawberry pink nails helps me feel good about myself even as I clutch the steering wheel, flip through paperwork, and wipe up messes.

Fit in a massage.
Drop in for a 15-minute walk-in chair massage at your local shopping mall for instant relief from tension headaches and tight muscles. Best of all, no appointments needed!

Escape into that guilty pleasure read.
I've always got at least one audiobook downloaded onto my phone for those endless hours of chauffeuring kids, sitting in waiting rooms, and idling in carpool.

Hire some help for everyday tasks.
Have a housekeeping service clean your bathrooms and kitchen every other week. Don't let lawn work be a time suck when there's an eager teenager in your neighborhood looking for pocket cash. These are both big bangs for your buck in terms of getting a little relief.

Just say 'no.'
Don't feel obligated to do extra activities or signup for volunteer work out of a sense of obligation. It's okay to prioritize yourself right now.

Ask for help that's actually helpful when friends and family offer.
Suggestions include: Would you bring by a meal on Tuesday? Could you drop my daughter off at piano lessons this afternoon? When you swing by would you bring a gallon of milk?

Limit time with naysayers.
Don't seek advice or support from people, even family members, who don't 'get' the very real challenges you're facing.

Join a support group.
Online support groups are a great way to feel less alone and get practical suggestions. Find my recommendations for online support groups in the Additional Resources section of this book.

Be your own greatest fan.
Be kind to yourself. Forgive yourself. Remind yourself of all the things you do well. Give yourself a generous 'A' for effort for those things you don't do so well.

Raising a child with RAD is overwhelming and usually the first thing to go is taking care of ourselves. To be successful, we need to build our resilience, increase our stress tolerance, and find ways to fit in self-care. Do it for your family, but especially do it for yourself.

Start small but start today.

CAREGIVERS NEED THERAPY TOO
Raising a child with RAD can be exhausting, demoralizing, frustrating, and painful.

One RAD parent says:

"My son is 11 and getting worse. He targets me and his cruelty is almost more than I can take."

It's 24/7, all consuming, and it seems to eat mothers alive. If you're a RAD mom, you will likely benefit from seeing a therapist for yourself.

When my son first went into residential treatment, I started seeing a therapist. She taught me a very simple breathing exercise.

Breathe in through your mouth, a single deep breath while counting to five.
(Breathe in: one – two – three – four – five)

Then,

Breathe out through your mouth, a single deep breath while counting down from five.
(Breathe out: five – four – three – two – one)

She told me to do this when I was in the car, lying in bed at night, making school lunches—anytime and anywhere I was feeling stressed. It was so simple, but in the years of chaos, I'd forgotten to breathe.

I was also able to vent in *my* therapist's office. Remember when I said to hold back with your child's therapist? Well, your own therapist is the place to let it all out. Find a therapist you feel comfortable with and get the support you need. If scheduling is a problem, look into the online options via Skype or Zoom for convenience.

If you've been struggling to raise a child with RAD for a while, you may want to consider being evaluated for PTSD. I developed this condition, as have many other moms of kids with RAD.

Lien says, "Post-traumatic stress disorder for parents of kids with RAD is a very real thing."

Common symptoms of PTSD include:

- Decreased interest in activities you used to enjoy

- Feeling emotionally out of control

- Heightened sense of anxiety, and

- Depression and feelings of low self-worth

You can find additional useful information on this from RAD Advocates in the Additional Resources section of this book.

You can also talk to your doctor about medications to help with anxiety or depression. They may feel that medication is needed to help take the edge off so you can cope.

ONLINE SUPPORT
It is difficult to find local families who are also raising a child with

RAD. One option is to join a closed Facebook group that offers community and support to parents of children with RAD.

These private groups are amazing places to get support, ask questions, and connect with other parents. As a bonus, you may find parents in your local area through these groups and be able to start in person friendships.

You'll find the online support groups I recommend in the Additional Resources section of this book.

While Facebook groups have moderators and do their best to maintain member's privacy, nothing online is truly private. Be cautious in what and how you post.

RAD MYTHS DISPELLED

Because it is rare and relatively unknown, there are many myths about RAD. These ideas are damaging to the child with the disorder and burdensome to their caregivers.

MYTH
ALL THEY NEED IS LOVE

Don't all kids need love? Of course. They need love, affection, and hugs to grow into healthy, well-adjusted adults. However, love—while important—won't cure a child who has RAD.

These children need very serious treatment and often medication in order to learn to cope with the world around them. By perpetuating this myth, an undue burden is put on caregivers who need to feel empowered to find outside help rather than believing they should be able to solve the problem on their own.

MYTH
KIDS GROW OUT OF RAD

RAD is not a phase kids simply grow out of. The permanent scars of trauma etched deep inside cannot be healed. Children who receive proper treatment can grow up to be healthy, successful adults. Others can at least learn to cope with the world and live within normal social boundaries. However, too many of these kids end up sucked into the criminal justice system. It's critical to understand that your child will not outgrow the condition and to get them help at an early age.

MYTH
ALL KIDS GO THROUGH PHASES LIKE THIS

Sure, many kids go through challenging phases as they develop and grow. However, the extreme behaviors of children with RAD are something else entirely.

These behaviors are not "normal" and cannot be managed in a "normal way." What works with other kids is very unlikely to work with a child who has RAD. This is why research and new treatments for RAD are desperately needed.

MYTH
I'M NOT BONDING WTH MY CHILD, I CAUSED THIS

When an adoptive parent or caregiver struggles to bond with their child, it's easy to feel responsible, but this is a bit of a chicken-and-egg dilemma. Are your child's behavioral problems caused by your difficulty with attaching to them? Or, are you struggling to attach to your child because of their behavioral problems? For parents who adopt children with RAD, it is the latter. It's important to remember that RAD is a pre-existing condition our children came to us with. Really getting your arms around this truth can go a long way towards releasing guilt and shame that keeps so many from seeking help.

MYTH
RAD IS A "FAKE" DIAGNOSIS

Currently, reactive attachment disorder is listed in the Diagnostic and Statistical Manual of Mental Disorders (DSM) alongside other disorders we are familiar with like, bipolar, ADHD, and schizophrenia. The DSM is the standard classification of mental disorders used world-wide by mental health professionals and the health insurance industry.

That said, there is much debate about the RAD diagnosis, in large part due to harmful attachment "therapies" associated with it in the past. Leading clinicians and researchers are promoting a shift towards Developmental Trauma Disorder (DTD) as a more comprehensive diagnosis for the impacts of early childhood trauma. Unfortunately, this was submitted for consideration as a new diagnosis in the most recent version of the DSM and was rejected. You can find a link to Kolk's journal article, "Developmental Trauma Disorder: Towards a Rational Diagnosis for Childhood Trauma Histories" in the Additional Resources section of this book for more information.

TEN UGLY TRUTHS YOU MUST KNOW

Parents of kids who are on the severe end of the RAD spectrum often feel as if they are living on the verge of a nervous breakdown. They are afraid, perhaps even terrified, of their children. They literally wonder how they'll make it through the next day. Some are suicidal. Many are depressed, fearful, and unable to cope.

Too many parents, years after their child is grown and gone, deeply regret sacrificing their other children, their marriages, and their mental health and well-being.

I've been there.

That's why I'm going to share with you 10 straightforward truths, one parent to another, that you're not going to find anywhere else. These are especially appropriate for parents of children who have become dangerous and violent.

So, let's strip away the platitudes and really talk about how to survive. Here are the unfiltered, pragmatic RAD-parent-to-RAD-parent truths you must know.

1 **If your child is exhibiting extreme behaviors that you can't safely deal with on your own, get your child into residential treatment as soon as possible.** Do whatever it takes. Go to the mental health ER every single time your child's behavior is dangerous to himself and others, even if it's every week or every other day. Your insurance company will be most likely to fund the treatment your child needs if they understand the gravity of the situation. Money talks. If they keep getting billed by the ER they'll be far more willing to approve the less costly (and more appropriate) treatment options.

If your child is violent towards you (Intentional Child on Parent Violence, I-CPV), you may need to press criminal charges.

2 Without highly specialized treatment, the child perpetrating the abuse will not get better. Far too often, it becomes necessary to have them institutionalized or incarcerated for the safety of their siblings, parents, and themselves. Yes, the justice system is unlikely to do them any good. But it may be the only option to keep everyone safe. Don't put your other children's safety or yours in jeopardy by waiting too long.

3 **Don't beat yourself up for not having natural affection and love towards your child.** You have been the victim of trauma akin to domestic violence and no one believes a victim should naturally feel affection toward her abuser. It's hard for us to think of children, even young grade school aged children, in these harsh terms, but that's the reality.

Lien says, "It's unreasonable to force a parent to bond with a child whose behaviors have led to his or her PTSD."

Your feelings are normal. What's not normal is the extreme situation you are going through.

4 **Be prepared for false allegations**. CPS will take seriously even absurd claims—yes, despite witnesses and video footage. And you absolutely can lose all your children during these investigations. If the allegations are substantiated you can lose them forever.

One RAD parent says:

"There is no 'innocent until proven guilty' with CPS. You can lose your other kids over an absurd, completely ridiculous lie told by a child you are trying to help."

If your child has started making false allegations against you, consider this a huge flashing warning sign. Act fast to get help and to get them into residential treatment.

5 **Enjoy your summer break and let siblings enjoy it too.** If that means setting your child with RAD up with a TV and game system, do it. What good are parenting ideals if you sacrifice siblings to reach them? Someday you'll look back on these years and be amazed at how you managed day-to-day. Be pragmatic and don't lose yourself in a losing battle.

6 **Your other children are being exposed to domestic violence.** Exposure to hours of screaming, explosive rages, and physical attacks is harmful to siblings. They are being forced to live in a state of hypervigilance that can cause anxiety, depression, PTSD, and so much more. It would be considered child abuse or neglect for a mother to allow their children to be exposed to similar behavior from partner domestic abuse. Find a way to protect siblings —they have rights too; you have an obligation to them too.

7 **Some children with RAD abuse their siblings.** They may bully younger siblings or abuse them physically, emotionally, or sexually. This is something you must keep a very close eye on. Remember children with RAD are extremely manipulative and this can enable them to abuse their siblings right under your nose.

8 **Realize that someday you may have to choose between protecting your non-RAD children and keeping your child who is exhibiting extreme, dangerous RAD behaviors at home.** This may mean putting your child in residential programs that seem to be little more than "holding cells." It may mean filing criminal charges against them. These are heartbreaking choices no parent should have to make, but they may be coming your way. Start preparing yourself now.

9 If it is necessary for your child to receive help in a residential treatment facility, understand that the experience may exacerbate your child's behavior, possibly making it worse. Your child will be exposed to children with worse behaviors, and many of the "treatments" will empower your child to continue with his behaviors. Despite this, these facilities are sometimes the best, the necessary, choice when you need to protect the child from himself and to keep siblings safe.

10 Your child's therapist and treatment team will turn on you. As the parent, you are an easy target and much easier to focus on than RAD. Also, providers need to show positive outcomes to continue receiving funding and some will skew the truth to do it. Always remember that this is your child's team, not yours.

LOVE ISN'T ENOUGH

It's a hard truth many parents of children with RAD, myself included, have had to face. No amount of love, no "forever family," can heal the wounds of early childhood trauma. Furthermore, the child welfare and mental health systems do not have solutions for children who desperately need families but aren't able to safely live in them.

Meanwhile, RAD is crippling our children—emotionally, socially, and mentally—and stealing their futures. It is destroying and breaking families. Unfortunately, moms are blamed and shamed into silence. As a result, their children don't get the help they need to grow and thrive. It is imperative that the mental health community acknowledge this urgent crisis and offer meaningful treatments for positive outcomes.

No matter how much you love your child, you cannot "fix" RAD. You alone cannot solve this. What you *can* do is be an advocate for your child. You *can* balance empathy and pragmatism. There are successes to be had if you put on your trauma-informed lens. Your child *can* do better. Your home *can* be more peaceful.

PROLOGUE

I surge out of my chair, my face flushing, and I can't keep the tremble out of my voice. "He's threatening to stab his little brother and strangle me. How can you still think he's safe to come home?"

"Devon is not a threat to anyone," Wanda says, with an exasperated sigh. Devon, my 11-year-old son, is in the psych ward because he claims he's seeing hallucinations of a man ordering him to stab his little brother and to strangle me. Wanda is his therapist.

The sour smell of the hospital hangs thick in the air and gums to the inside of my mouth as I look around the table at the social worker, the nurse, and Wanda. Devon is using these "hallucinations" to threaten me. Can't any of them see that?

"You need to be supportive of what is in Devon's best interest," Wanda says.

I sink back into my chair and months of family therapy lurch through my mind. I know Wanda thinks Devon's behaviors are my fault and that I'll try to use this latest hospitalization to keep him from moving back home.

Panic curls its fingers around my throat.

Wanda is right.

I'll do whatever it takes to keep him from coming home.

1
(8 years earlier)

"As far as foster kids go, they're pretty much perfect," says Tina, a state of Florida adoption worker. "Makayla is two and Devon is three. Devon's such a bright, funny, handsome young man. And Makayla loves to wear dresses and have her hair done."

As her words fan my long-held dreams to adopt, I gaze out of my office window at the palm trees shading the parking lot and Devon and Makayla form like mirages in my imagination.

Tina lowers her voice, like a friend taking me into her confidence. "Since they're so young and haven't been abused, there are several other prospective families interested in them. But we want to find the right family. I know y'all recently decided not to adopt, but we're hoping you might reconsider?"

I eagerly agree, wondering how this unsolicited call could be anything but fate.

"We think you're a good match for a couple of reasons. You have other children, so we know you can handle a sibling group. Not everyone can." There's an awkward pause. "Also, I understand you're a mixed-race family?"

"Yes. I'm white and my husband is black. He's Jamaican."

"That's perfect. Devon and Makayla have a white mom. They have different dads, but both dads are black. It's so important to place kids in families where they look like they fit."

Whether Tina knows it or not, this is an issue close to my heart. My stepson, Sam, has a dark complexion like his dad. After taking in my freckles and fair skin, strangers often ask him if I'm his "real" mom. So, I get it. Kids shouldn't have to deal with that.

"When can we meet them?" I ask.

"We really don't like to showcase children. We used to do these adoption fairs …" her voice trails off without completing the thought. "Anyway, the kids end up hurt and disappointed when they aren't chosen."

I understand, but I'm still surprised they're asking us to make such an important decision, a lifelong decision, without even meeting the kids first.

As though reading my mind, Tina adds in a sing-song, "Remember, we don't get to meet our birth children before we commit to them."

Coiling the phone cord around my finger, I venture, "But they're so little. Can't you tell them it's a play date?" As Tina's indecisive pause stretches, self-conscious words jumble out of my mouth in my rush to not be misunderstood. "It's not that I want to see what they look like or anything like that. It's just that we tried to adopt a little boy a few months ago. His name was Eli. It … it didn't work out."

"That's why you asked to be taken off the adoption list?"

"Yes." I sway into my desk chair, unable to put the grief of our failed adoption into words. Having to send Eli back into "the system" was devastating and I still haven't gotten over the heartbreak and the guilt. "We can't jump in again without at least meeting the kids first."

"Well," Tina says, drawing out the word thoughtfully, "let me talk to my supervisor and see if I can't arrange for a short, little visit."

We hang up and my fingers tremble with excitement as I dial my husband's extension. Delano and I are both employed by the same company. I work upstairs as a project manager and he works downstairs in the warehouse. I hear a forklift beeping in the background when he answers my call.

"You're not going to believe it," I gush. "I just got a call to see if we'll adopt a little girl and boy. They're two and three." As I go on, Delano takes it in stride, not surprised I'm once again talking about foster care and adoption. After all, it's how we met.

Back when I was single, long before meeting Delano, I'd scrolled through face after face of smiling foster children on the AdoptUS website. I was especially drawn to the sibling groups whose only wish was to be adopted together. I was still in my early twenties and single. I was afraid adoption agencies wouldn't consider me qualified to be an adoptive parent so I signed up to foster instead.

My longest placement—over six months—was for two sisters. Taylor was eight with the cheekbones of a runway model. Laila, six, had frizzy hair and spindly arms and legs. Both girls told me I was way too young to be a foster parent, and they were probably right. While my friends were out dating and going to parties, I was learning how to parent on-the-job.

We spent long hours on South Florida's beaches and went to many events hosted by the mega-church I fostered through. I drove them to school every morning because I didn't like the look of the bus stop, even though the case worker assured me it was safe. It was also my responsibility to supervise weekly visitations with their parents, and to comfort them after each visit when all they wanted was to go home to their mommy. Laila often wet the bed for the couple of days following these visits. I surprised myself with the ease at which I was able to manage cleaning up after this. However, my apartment didn't have a washer or dryer, so there was no escaping Saturday morning trips to the laundromat.

One morning, I was folding our clothes while the girls sat on flimsy plastic chairs eating gummy bears. They were watching a cartoon on the TV that was mounted on a wall in one corner of the facility. A friendly little boy with a toothy smile came running out of the office to watch with them. The manager, my future husband Delano, had a muscular build and a wide smile with perfect teeth. "That's my son, Sam," he said in a soft Jamaican accent. He pointed to the boy who was howling with laughter at the cartoon and had theatrically rolled out of his seat. Sam's mother had passed away and Delano was a widower. "He's six. About the same age as your daughters?" he asked.

"They're six and eight," I said. Not wanting to leave any false impressions, I added, "But, they're not mine."

His eyes widened. "I see you here every Saturday. You're so kind to them. Like they're your own children."

"They're sweet girls," I said, ducking my head.

The next time we saw Sam, I asked if he could spend the afternoon with us, knowing the laundromat couldn't be a fun Saturday for any kid. Delano agreed, suggesting we come by his apartment later that evening for dinner. That's how I found myself face-to-face with Jamaican chicken foot soup.

Sam put one boney chicken foot in his mouth, demonstrating how to suck the meat off. Taylor and Laila, who could never get enough to eat, followed Sam's example, slurping and smacking their lips. When I snuck my two chicken feet into Laila's bowl, Sam caught my eye and gave me a precocious wink. Later that evening, when we said goodbye, Sam stroked my long, straight hair and offered me the top of his head in return. I gamely ran my palm over his tiny curls. Seeing this, Taylor yanked me toward the parking lot with a scowl. It was the first of many "dates" Delano and I had with our kids in tow.

By the time Taylor and Laila returned to live with their mom, I had become quite attached to them. I'd always known they'd leave, but never expected it to hurt so much. I only took short-term foster care placements after that, because I couldn't bear to get my heart tangled up again.

When Delano and I married some months later, he and Sam moved into my apartment, and Sam took over my foster care bedroom. To foster again, Delano and I would have to reapply together, so I put that dream on hold and focused on my new role as Sam's mom. A year later, Delano and I had a child together. We named him Amias which means "loved." We went on to get licensed to foster children together, and I never stopped dreaming of blending adopted kids into our family.

Now, two years later, I'm clutching the phone, eagerly telling Delano about Devon and Makayla and how my adoption dreams may finally be coming true.

I look up when my coworker Pat raps on the glass of my office door. I end my call with Delano and wave her in. Frustrated energy hums around her wiry frame and she shoves a hand through her short, gray hair. "I just wanted to make sure you saw the request I emailed you yesterday?"

"Oh, it's all done," I say.

"Done?" Pat barks a surprised laugh.

I smile. "I know you're under a lot of pressure, so I took care of it first thing this morning."

As her body visibly unwinds into my guest chair, Pat says, "I'd say, 'Add it to my tab,' but I think I owe you more than a coffee for this one!"

Our visit with Devon and Makayla is in a musty room in the bowels of a Department of Children and Families (DCF) building. Not wanting to raise Amias and Sam's hopes, we've left them home with a babysitter.

Piles of shabby toys lie strewn across the floor, and there's a faded pink and white plastic kitchenette set against one wall. Devon and Makayla are already inside the room. We go in and sit on the floor while Tina and another DCF worker pull up folding chairs outside the door.

Makayla stands, holding a limp cloth doll, and stares at us with her mouth open. She has huge, round eyes. Purple barrettes that match her dress dangle from the ends of her long braids.

Devon grins at us, pink cheeks rounding against his honey-brown complexion. He's got the kind of face that can charm anyone, and he's sure out to charm us. He tugs at my sleeve, and I watch him move a chunky plastic truck along the floor as he makes putt-putt noises. I fiddle with my silver hoop earrings, enchanted, as he shows me how he can stack blocks into a tower. I glance at Delano to see if he's watching, but he's holding out a Barbie doll to Makayla.

"Here sweetie. Do you want this baby doll?" he coaxes.

"Wook, wook." Devon bumps a toy block against my face. I smile and reach up to steady him, surprised by how solid he is.

Delano pretends to drink from a pink plastic teacup before holding it out to Makayla. "No," she growls, keeping her distance. I can't help but feel drawn to this little warrior girl who refuses to make sweet with strangers.

When our short visit is over, Tina's colleague takes the kids by their hands and leads them out of the room. Makayla doesn't give us a backward glance, but Devon beams over his shoulder and waves to us for as long as he can. I wave back until they turn the corner and are out of sight.

"Makayla is normally very friendly," Tina says, worrying her beaded bracelet. "I'm not sure why she was acting like that. She might have been tired or hungry. I hope y'all won't decide not to adopt them because of this." She fixes us with an expectant look. They've accommodated our request for a visit—against policy—and now it's time for our decision.

Delano nods almost imperceptibly and I already know my answer. Devon is friendly and easygoing. Amias will love having him for a brother. Makayla is going to be a handful for sure, but I love her spunk.

As we walk toward the exit, Delano laces his fingers through mine. Tina goes over the next steps for Devon and Makayla to acclimate to the family before moving into our home. As she tells us they'll remain foster children for three months before the adoption can be finalized, my heart snags on a memory. We didn't make it through the same mandatory waiting period last time. Sending Eli back broke something inside of me. I can't go through that—can't do that to a child—ever again.

2

Delano strides through the garage, clenching a roll of paper towels in one hand. His accent is usually melodic, but when he's upset his dialect runs thick and fast. Right now, he's upset. He's sure one of our neighbor's dogs peed on the concrete floor. I point out that the garage door has been closed all day, but he pays me no mind. "Me keep telling the man to keep him dog over him house."

I sigh, knowing this will only fuel his war with our neighbors over their unruly Rottweilers who constantly defecate on our lawn. To my embarrassment, Delano scoops up the poop and flings it onto their front yard. I'm not particularly concerned about the dogs, because they're just a nuisance and not dangerous.

"Me can't take this," he rants. "Keri, you have to do something about this. You hear me? You-hear-me-Keri?"

The whole neighborhood probably hears him, but I've got more important things to worry about. I go back inside the house, through the kitchen, and to the living room. Standing outside of the door, I peek in. There's a loveseat, shelves, and toy bins against the walls. The room—heated by the Florida sun through two large windows—is toasty, but the kids don't seem to notice.

I watch two-year-old Amias pull a plastic Dalmatian puppy across the floor by its cord. Its tail wags as its red nose blinks, and it plays jaunty music. Devon jostles Amias, pushing closer to the action, and Makayla shows off dimples that I hadn't noticed before. Amias has a chocolate fingerprint smear up the side of his tee-shirt, and Devon has a white powder mustache.

After we'd agreed to adopt Devon and Makayla, DCF had wasted no time. We had two more short visits, and, less than a month after meeting them, here they are. Of course, our fostering license was in order, and there weren't many preparations to make: the house is childproofed and a tall, wooden fence surrounds our grassy backyard. When we moved in, the first thing we did was tear out the previous owner's above-ground pool. Sam had grumbled as we dismantled and carried one of his long-held childhood dreams to the curb. But, with Amias beginning to toddle about, a pool seemed too risky.

Devon and Makayla are sharing what was Amias' bedroom. It's not a problem, because Amias co-sleeps with us. Delano and I are already planning to move into a larger house once we finalize the adoption. We'll need more bedrooms, and, judging from the toys scattered all over the living room floor, we need a playroom too.

I pick stuffed animals up off of the floor and place them in a plastic bin. Smoothing one doll's long, blond hair and straightening its dress, I say, "Makayla, this doll is ..."

"Kayla."

It takes a moment to realize she's asking—well, more like ordering—me to call her "Kayla" instead of "Makayla." I put a smile in my voice. "Kayla, sweetheart, this doll is for you. Isn't she pretty?" She doesn't reach for the doll, so I set it on the shelf.

I ease onto one arm of the loveseat to watch them play. Kayla, not yet stretched tall like the boys, is chubby with eyes as round as marbles. Amias is three months older than Kayla and a year younger than Devon. He has looser, darker curls and a wide smile. He's a string bean, unlike Devon, who is husky. The tallest of the three, Devon has low, golden curls. Even so, at first glance, just as Tina had hoped, the three kids could easily pass for biological siblings.

...

On Devon and Kayla's first day of daycare since moving in, my eyes snap open before my alarm clock buzzes. The tasks for the morning are ticking through my mind. I don't wear makeup and I simply run a brush through my hair before pulling on jeans and a black, V-neck top.

Delano has left a load of folded laundry on the machine. I sort through and find pink shorts and a white t-shirt with a florescent pink flower for Kayla. I pick out a pair of jean shorts and a Blue's Clues shirt for Devon. After rousing everyone from bed, I pour myself a cup of coffee and gather the "little kids" in the living room to help with their buttons, zippers, and shoelaces. Sam, quite a bit older, takes care of getting himself ready in the mornings.

Amias and Kayla determinedly, albeit slowly, dress themselves. Devon holds out his shirt to me. "You're a big boy. You can do it," I say, with enthusiasm that would rival a brand-new preschool teacher. After a moment's hesitation, he pushes a foot through one sleeve of the shirt. His dark eyes, hooded by long lashes, watch me watching him.

Poor thing, he's almost four and he doesn't know how to dress himself. I motion him to me, and slip the shirt over his head. "See? Easy peasy." Devon puts his soft pudgy hands on either side of my face and rewards me with a bright smile.

I pick up his shorts and put them on his head like a hat. "Oops. That's not right. Hmmm. Do you know where they should go?" His sweet giggle burrows towards my heart. He snatches the shorts off his head and pulls them up his legs and on. "Good job," I say encouragingly. "Put on your socks next." When he turns away, I begin to straighten Kayla's plastic bow barrettes in her mounds of curly hair.

Then, Devon sneezes. One. Big. Sneeze. His hands hang limp at his sides as snot strings down over his lips and chin. He licks it. I gag and rush to get a package of baby wipes.

Sam snickers from the nearby table where he's eating cereal. "Awe, mom hates that stuff," he tells Devon.

I quickly clean Devon up so we won't be late.

Sam normally walks to the elementary school, which is a few blocks away. We wave goodbye to him as we pull out of the driveway and head for Little Rascal's, the daycare center where DCF has enrolled Devon and Kayla. It's close to our house, but I've never liked the look of it. From the outside, it's dingy, and the side alley has been poorly retrofitted into a concrete play area.

Delano waits in the car with Amias while I take Devon and Kayla inside. As I open the main door, I recoil from the sour smell of cleaning chemicals and dirty diapers. Devon tugs at my hand to pull away. I crouch to hug him and he stiffens in my arms. "Have a good day," I say, before releasing him. He turns and runs to the table where staff are serving breakfast.

I tuck Kayla's dangling braids behind her ears. She clutches my arm. "You're not goin' anywhere," she demands, screwing up her face. I kneel and point out a dollhouse and a reading area, but she refuses to budge. "You're. Not. Goin'. Anywhere," she punches out.

On second glance, the reading area isn't all that appealing. The vinyl bean bag chair has cracks, and the books look grimy and old. I spend some time trying to comfort Kayla and to get her interested in toys.

One of the daycare workers notices my dilemma and lumbers over. She pries Kayla's fingers off my arm and tells her they'll go have breakfast. Kayla looks at me with furious eyes. My stomach clenches at the thought of walking away. I look over and see Devon earnestly eating his cereal. "I'll be back soon," I promise as I give Kayla a hug and a kiss on her soft cheek.

Our next stop is Amias' preschool, King's Kids. It's a clean, spacious building with a modern playground visible through spanning windows. Unfortunately, they don't have a contract with DCF which is why Devon and Kayla can't come here too.

Amias' teacher, Ms. Angelica, is petite with auburn hair and a sweet smile. As I'm leaving his classroom, Amias plays one of his favorite games, teasing me that he might love "Miss 'Gelica" more than he loves me. His pants are twisted from dressing himself, and I tug on the elastic waist to straighten them. As I do, I fake cry and make a sad face until he smothers me with kisses. "I love you most, Mommy," he says.

Once at work, I try to focus on tasks I'm normally passionate about—updating project plans, writing business requirements, and reviewing vendor proposals—but I can't concentrate. Instead, I'm jotting down a mental to-do list: grocery shopping, a few things to pick up at Walmart, call the caseworker back to schedule our first home visit, fax documents to the adoption lawyer …

…

On Saturday we wind our way through the Swap Shop, a sprawling indoor-outdoor flea market where vendors hawk everything from knockoff designer handbags to cell phones. We find a Caribbean hair shop and Delano haggles over a price. In a heavy Dominican accent, the friendly woman promises us braids that will last at least six to eight weeks.

As Kayla takes a seat on a tall stool, the boys head for the arcade and food court with Delano. Miffed, Kayla folds her arms over her chest and clamps her mouth into a frown. Her hair reaches down to her lower back, and it takes close to two hours for the woman to undo the current braids and then create new braids. When they're finished, with pink and purple beads on the ends, she holds up a mirror for Kayla to admire herself, but Kayla only scowls.

I leave a generous tip.

We meet the boys near the exit. They're all smiles, having played games and eaten carnival foods. Delano has a bowl of mango chunks that he's bought for Kayla. She eagerly takes them, giving him a huge smile.

I take Devon's hand, stopping his twirling, and we lead the way to the parking lot.

"Did you have fun?" I ask.

Devon bobs his head and his cheeks round with freckles as he grins up at me.

"What did you do?"

I'm pretty sure what he's saying is that he had a Coke slushy. His words are jumbled and somewhat incoherent, but I'm mostly able to work out what he says. Devon is a year older than Amias and Kayla, but his speech is babyish, like a much younger child. He can be hard to understand, but the more I talk with him, the better I'm getting at it. He pulls at my hand as he half walks, half bounces beside me like Tigger. I need to make sure Delano knows that Coke is full of caffeine and sugar.

The beads on Kayla's braids clink and chatter as she stomps past the lines of parked cars. By the time we reach our vehicle, she's tugging at the braids and scratching her scalp. I sweep her hands away and tell her how pretty they are. How pretty *she* is.

"Her ears are too hard," Delano says, and he's right. She's one stubborn girl.

The next day, Sunday morning, I sit on the couch with my legs curled beneath me and my coffee cup on the side table. My mind flits back to my early twenties, when foster care adoption was only a far-fetched dream. In the quiet of the house, I journal about how Devon is so gentle and sweet. I can sense the softness inside of him. Kayla is harder, like she's got a chip on her shoulder, and she acts much older than she is.

Kayla stalks into the room. One side of her hair is a frizzy mess. The other side is still braided, but her fingers are busy at work. I can't help but chuckle in resignation. "Someone didn't get much sleep last night," I say, and motion her to me. I push my journal beneath a couch cushion and cuddle her onto my lap to help her undo the rest of those "ouchie" braids.

After breakfast, I settle in to work on Kayla's hair. I sit on the couch behind her, and she sits on a pillow on the floor. Combs, gels, elastic bands, and hair bobbles litter the coffee table. I twist small locks of hair into simple three-strand braids while she watches *Elmo's World*. One of my friends taught me how to properly care for African American hair back when I had foster children, but I realize that I'll have to ask her about Kayla's hair, because it's curly with a fine texture.

Meanwhile, Devon is in the bathroom trying to use the potty "like a big boy." I'd been surprised that both Devon, almost four, and Kayla, two-and-a-half, were wearing diapers when they came to us.

We took them to Walmart so they could pick out undies. Devon had chosen briefs with doggie paws but only reluctantly wears them. He prefers GoodNites, diapers that pull on like underwear, but I only let him wear those at night.

Devon hasn't had any accidents at Little Rascal's, so he is at least partially potty trained. Delano makes sure that Devon uses the bathroom before he goes to bed, but he still has accidents most nights. It's odd. The sheets are pee-soaked, but his GoodNites are dry. Maybe he's too nervous to use the bathroom in a new house. I remember Eli also wetting the bed at night, and he was a few years older than Devon.

Sitting back, I admire my braids. Adorable. But Kayla does not think so. Despite what Tina told me, I'm finding that Kayla hates getting her hair done, pretty barrettes, dresses, or anything "girly." On our Walmart trip, she'd picked out superhero undies from the boy's aisle for herself. Following Amias' example, she wears them backwards so she can see the picture that's meant to be splashed across her bottom. I'm not sure why she was in diapers when she came to us, because she hasn't had a single accident.

Four braids later, I stand to check on Devon. There's an encouraging smile already on my face as I turn the corner into the bathroom.

I see Devon sitting on the edge of the bathtub. His arm is elbow deep in the toilet. Horrified, I move toward him.

Then, I see the poop in his hand.

I clap my hand over my mouth, and my stomach lurches.

DISCLAIMER

I am thankful to all those who have contributed to my knowledge and understanding of RAD and its treatment. The information contained in this guide is based on my own experiences. This guide cannot substitute for professional advice based on the circumstances of any particular family.

I have been in contact with hundreds of parents and found our experiences to be uncannily similar. On occasion, with permission, I anonymously share the stories and quotes of other parents. My children have given their permission for me to include the information about our family that I have in this book. In all other instances, any similarity to the stories and experiences of others is coincidental.

Made in United States
Troutdale, OR
08/31/2024

22423318R00066